To Learn How to Teach English

With Practical Classroom Activities

OKITA, Yoshio

Kwansei Gakuin University Press

To Haruka

PREFACE

This book is designed to provide opportunities for English language teachers who are too occupied with daily work to reflect on their teaching. Every teacher hopes to improve their teaching skills and techniques, but many do not have enough time to do so.

Teachers must be fully aware that everything around us has changed very rapidly (e.g., society, technology, cultural values, human interests). This is also the case with the attitudes towards and expectations of English learning and teaching. Today many teachers may find themselves at sea when they realize that the methodologies under which they learned English differ from what is in demand today.

Many non-native English teachers learned English in a traditional way that focused on grammar, translation, memorization and receptive language skills. For them, studying the language was synonymous with expanding their knowledge about the language. This is mainly because in many countries they learned English in middle school in preparation for university entrance examinations.

This book is also intended for those novice teachers who wish to make a significant breakthrough in designing classroom exercises to foster students' communicative skills in English.

After spending a few years in a pre-service teachers' training course and studying recent trend in communicative language learning and teaching, they embark on their teaching careers. Then, they come to realize the gap between what the board of education expects them to do and what is still taking place in most schools.

Some are lucky enough to remember one or two communicative activities from their university courses and have students perform them. On the surface, this system works perfectly. However, even the best activity will be less engaging when students are asked to do it for the fifth time, as much of an activity's value is in its novelty. Others may continue the same routine classwork wondering if it is worthy to be called "communicative," that is, if it has any relevancy to developing practical language skills. There is no one available to provide them with any suggestions or advice. Some senior teachers may only give quizzical glances.

The sample activities in each chapter are classified according to the language skill which each of them is basically concerned with. In some situations, two or more skills (e.g., listening, speaking, reading, and writing) may be involved. Where this is the case, the criterion of grouping is based on the skill that is primarily emphasized.

Not all the ideas discussed in each chapter are equally suited to all cases. Obviously, many will have to be modified to fulfill the needs in specific teaching environments. It is hoped that exercises described in the subsequent chapters will act as a catalyst to inspire teachers to develop their existing expertise in teaching English.

Some of the ideas in this book have evolved from conversations with the author's colleagues and friends at professional meetings. Others have been widely disseminated in various forms over the years and put into practice in class. Still others are adaptations and modifications of those obtained from multiple information sources listed in the references sections.

In this book, the personal pronoun for the teacher is "she" and "he" (used alternately by chapter) to indicate the fact that teachers are of both sexes, without any intended significance.

Good luck on your English teaching!

Author's note

I would like to express my appreciation and thanks to Alex Hayashi and two anonymous reviewers for careful proofreading and helpful suggestions.

TABLE OF CONTENTS

PREFACE 3

CHAPTER ONE
On Listening 9

§1 **Acquisition-oriented listening activities and inductive language learning** ——————————————— 9
   1 Total Physical Response
   2 "Simon Says"

§2 **Types of learning-oriented listening** ——————— 12
   1 Bottom-up listening
   2 Dictation
   3 Top-down listening
   4 Task listening

CHAPTER TWO
On Speaking 27

§1 **The audio-lingual method** ——————————— 27

§2 **Communicative Language Teaching** ——————— 28

§3 **Communicative competence** ——————————— 28
   1 Linguistic competence
   2 Sociolinguistic competence
   3 Discourse competence
   4 Strategic competence
   5 The challenge of teaching communicative competence in the classroom

§4 **Classroom activities to foster communicative competence** ——————————————————— 31
   1 Pattern practice
   2 Information gap activities
   3 Role-play
   4 Speeches

CHAPTER THREE
On Reading 47

- §1 **Bottom-up and top-down reading approaches** —— 47
  1. Grammar Translation Method
  2. The bottom-up reading approach
  3. The top-down reading approach and schema theory
  4. Interactive reading

- §2 **Three-stage reading activities** —— 52
  1. Background
  2. Components of the three-stage reading approach

- §3 **Rapid reading** —— 56
  1. Skimming through the paragraph-reading approach
  2. Scanning
  3. Differences between skimming and scanning

CHAPTER FOUR
On Writing 63

- §1 **From composition to communicative writing** —— 63
  1. Composition or writing?
  2. Criteria for accessing writing assignments
  3. From teacher-directed to student-directed writing

- §2 **Authenticity** —— 75

- §3 **The process and product approaches** —— 76
  1. The process approach in contrast to product approach
  2. Three components of process approach

CHAPTER FIVE
On Pronunciation 83

- §1 **General American English and Received Pronunciation** —— 83

- §2 **Segmental or suprasegmental?** —— 84
  1. Segmental features
  2. Suprasegmental features

- §3 **Sound modifications** —— 96
  1. Flapping
  2. Linking
  3. Assimilation
  4. Jokes to illustarate sound modifications

CHAPTER SIX
On Integration 101

§1 Using a course book ——————————101
1 Asking questions in pairs
2 A post-reading activity
3 Impersonation of a main character

§2 Beyond a course book ——————————105
1 Using a comic strip
2 Applying for an EFL program
3 Newspaper reporting
4 Postcard writing
5 Conducting a survey
6 Group research project
7 Debate

CHAPTER SEVEN
Vocabulary Games 115
1 Pictograph
2 Odd one out
3 Hidden commonalities
4 Animal grid
5 Spelling bee
6 Charades
7 Scrambled words
8 Missing vowels
9 Secret code
10 Key words
11 Words within a word
12 Matching symbols with meanings

CHAPTER EIGHT
Classroom Dynamics 127

§1 Optimal use of the board ——————————127
1 Purposes of board writing
2 Effective use of the board

§2 Teacher talk ——————————130
1 Eliciting
2 Questioning strategies

§3 Pair work and group work ——————————138
1 Chief functions
2 Side benefits

       3 Points to be observed
  §4 Four types of test evaluations —————————141
       1 Placement tests
       2 Diagnostic tests
       3 Achievement tests
       4 Proficiency tests

REFERENCES 143

INDEX 146

ACTIVITIES INDEX 148

On Listening

Learners' listening skills had long been kept in the background in language learning and teaching. A main reason for this may be the fleeting nature of sound, which could have made teachers believe that it is difficult to teach effective listening. Yet, since the 1980s, with attention centered on functional rather than literal language use, interest began to grow in ways to increase aural skills in learners.

In fact, listening is considered to be a skill with more practical usage in daily life than speaking, reading, or writing. Researchers suggest that the time spent on listening is double of that on speaking, four times of that on reading, and five times of that on writing. Graphically, ratios of time spent on each component can be illustrated in the pie chart below.

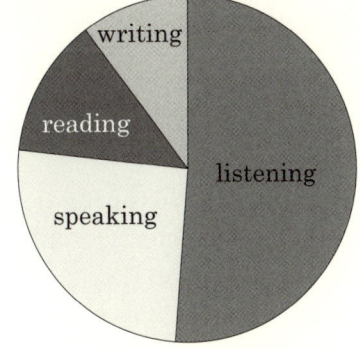

Ratios of time spent on the four langauage skills in daily life

In this chapter, we divide listening activities in English classes into two categories—acquisition-oriented and learning-oriented listening—and discuss each of these in detail.

§1 Acquisition-oriented listening activities and inductive language learning

The goal of **acquisition-oriented listening** activities is to train students to comprehend language items (e.g., grammar, vocabulary, and sentences) through their ears almost as naturally and instinctively as young children acquire their mother tongue. The assumption is that learners acquire those items without any strain and can, hopefully, apply them to practical use in a meaningful context, or the one with real-life and personal relevance to learners.

The essential point of the acquisition-oriented listening activity is that target language items are inductively introduced to students. This notion is described below.

Words and grammatical structures can be presented in two ways during class: either deductively or inductively. **Deductively**, the teacher usually introduces those target items in the students' mother tongue or first language **(L1)**. **Inductively**, this introduction is made in the target language.

In explaining lexical and structural elements in the target language, the teacher provides familiar, illustrative, and authentic examples for the students. This is often done with the help of pictures and **realia** (objects and materials from everyday life used as teaching aids), so that students will generalize the rules on their own more easily and naturally.

Such inductive instruction is more of a discovery activity for students and affords the chance to foster their language awareness. While the focus is on the messages that are being orally conveyed, they unconsciously learn the target structures or vocabulary words through listening. This is exactly what occurs in a stress-free L1 acquisition, and inductive foreign or second language **(L2)** learning appears to share these merits.

In fact, there are strong advocates for providing ample listening opportunities in an L2 setting. They take into account that language acquisition is enhanced by receiving extensive exposure to input-rich environments. Therefore, the teachers are expected to use the target language frequently when explaining language usage, clarifying directions, or exchanging small talk in class.

That explains acquisition-oriented listening in reference to inductive language learning. The following are perfect examples of this type of listening without causing too much pressure on the learners.

1 Total Physical Response

001: Total Physical Response

First:
The teacher gives and enacts oral commands, such as "Run," "Walk," and "Turn around." While she is doing this, students listen, watch her carefully, and imitate her actions.

Second:
She gives the same commands without a performance.

Students do as indicated without the benefit of her model.

The first step may be repeated a few times before proceeding to the second step. This is what is widely known as **Total Physical Response (TPR)** and is a good example of an acquisition-oriented listening activity. TPR was developed in the 1960s to help learners acquire the target language as naturally and easily as they did their native language. The teacher's role is that of a director.

Although the commands in the example above are uncomplicated, they can also be more complex, such as "Take a deep breath. Hold it. Exhale slowly," or "Go to the blackboard at the front of the classroom and draw a triangle in the lower bottom corner."

At the primary level, a TPR activity is often accompanied by a song. A good example is the song of "Head, shoulders, knees, and toes," in which young children sing while performing kinesthetic exercises.

A careful observation of children's first language acquisition shows that listening comprehension comes before all the other language behaviors: speaking, reading, and writing. What children hear becomes contextually meaningful and understandable. Young children can understand extremely complex utterances, even though they can only produce simple speech. What occurs here is natural and instinctive to them. This observation is the rationale behind TPR.

Furthermore, research suggests that even older students remember new words and phrases better, for example, action words when they are presented through physical involvement. This process is less demanding for learners than learning a language logically. (Note: In the activities described, hereafter, "T" stands for teacher, and "S" stands for student.)

2 "Simon Says"

002: "Simon Says"

T: Class, we are going to play "Simon Says." I am going to give you some orders. Please follow them. But there is a rule. You will do as I tell you to only when I say "Simon Says" at the beginning of each order. If you follow my order without my saying "Simon Says," you will be out of the game. Okay, let's start! Everybody, stand up!

Ss: *(Some do and some don't.)*

T: Oh, Oh... I see some students standing up. Sorry, you are out. Okay? Simon says, "Stand up!" Oh, Oh. Some of you are still sitting. This time...

"Simon Says" is a mildly competitive fun game based on the key concept of TPR and can be played by learners of all ages.

As seen above, participants cannot continue the game any longer if they follow instructions not preceded by "Simon Says" or fail to respond to those given after "Simon Says." The winner is the last person who has followed all the orders without any errors.

Command chains, such as "Simon Says, 'Raise your right hand.' Raise your left hand too," and "Simon Says, 'Turn around.' Simon Says, 'Keep on turning.' Okay, stop it," can be very misleading and confusing. If the teacher "catches" a student for raising his/her left hand or stopping turning, that student is eliminated from the game. Additionally, if the teacher says, "Stand up!" without "Simon Says" and she stands up (students should not do so), most of them are sure to be deceived.

Variations
- The teacher may give orders followed by phrases such as "Do this!" and "Do that!" (Orders after "Do this!" should be followed, and ones after the latter should not.)
- Students can take the teacher's role and give directions to others. Not only can this make the activity more amusing, but it also gives them speaking practice. In this case, the teacher acts as judge and rules out students who make mistakes.

In this section so far, the advantages of acquisition-oriented listening have been emphasized, but that should not discredit another type of listening: learning-oriented listening. This type of listening can also be fully exploited, especially in large classroom settings with students having the same first language, or when total amount of time allotted for the course is limited. In the next section, learning-oriented listening is addressed in detail.

§2 Types of learning-oriented listening

Learning-oriented listening activities primarily aim at examining or improving learners' listening abilities. This type of listening activity often takes the form of quizzes or exercises that are less probable in first language acquisition, except in special cases. A typical learning-oriented listening activity will be the following. Now observe and identify what the problem is.

003: A conventional learning-oriented activity

Students listen to a recorded short passage once or twice, and try to answer related questions that follow, either true-or-false or multiple-choice type.

Instead of using a recording, the teacher may read a passage aloud, monitoring the silent but important reactions from students. In this manner, she would know from their reactions which **lexical items** (words or phrases) may be beyond their level or difficult to hear. She then pronounces them more clearly or slowly, or even paraphrases them, in the second reading. Thus, using the teacher's own voice would definitely be a better choice. However, there is another problem yet to be solved.

What often occurs here is that listeners may have forgotten some minute facts by the time the questions are given. They may feel that this is a test of memorization or guessing ability rather than a helpful task for honing listening skills. Such classwork bears little or no relationship to real-life listening skills, and could only hinder their willingness to study English.

Learning-oriented listening may be grouped into the following three types for convenience, though categorizing them may sometimes be difficult:

- bottom-up listening;
- top-down listening;
- task listening.

In **bottom-up listening**, listeners' attention is directed toward individual lexical items, or sometimes toward more specific speech features, such as phonemes and intonation patterns.

In **top-down listening**, listeners seek more general information leading to prediction of the content, and here their previous knowledge carries weight.

Task listening requires further action from students based on the information obtained from listening.

1 Bottom-up listening

004: Bottom-up listening (1/7)
("-ed" pronunciations)

Students listen as the teacher reads the following pairs of verbs with an "-ed" ending written on the board. They then identify a pair(s) in which "-ed" is pronounced in the same or different way.

This is a perfect example of bottom-up listening, where students' attention will be kept on how **past tense morphemes** ("-ed") are pronounced. The exercise can be used to raise consciousness of the different sounds they make and why they occur. The teacher should refrain from showing those words in written form before pronouncing them. Otherwise, students would not focus on sounds.

💬 Variations

- A set of three words with "-ed" ending can be given and students determine which ending is pronounced differently from the other two, or spot the odd one out.
- This activity can be adapted to highlighting the differences among other pairs of words with similar (or targeted) vowels or consonants in them.

005: Bottom-up listening (2/7)
(stressed and unstressed words)

Students read aloud a given sentence or two, and guess which words in them will be pronounced with a stress and which will not. They then listen to the model reading, and confirm or refute their predictions.

To check their guesses, students concentrate on individual words. This is an excellent activity for making learners mindful of the differences between content words (usually stressed) and function words (usually unstressed). The activity also serves as a good introduction to the stress-timed features of the English sound system and helps students produce sentences with the appropriate English rhythm. For details, see page 91.

This activity can be applied to focus on other speech features of English, such as intonation patterns; students read sentences written on the board, predict if the sentences end in rising or falling intonation, and then listen to a model reading to examine their predictions.

006: Bottom-up listening (3/7)
(filling the blanks)

Students listen to the following famous **nursery rhyme** from a recording and fill in blanks in the worksheet with the words they hear.

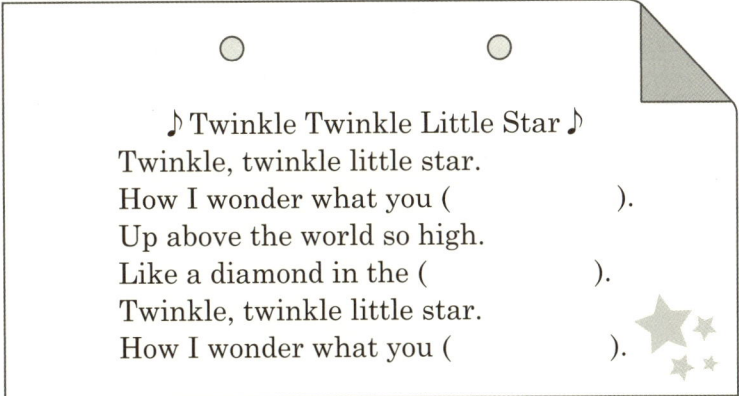

In this standard bottom-up listening activity, students attend to individual words and fill out blanks in the text while listening. The blanks should be set according to which words the teacher emphasizes unless otherwise specifically designed. Words to be filled in may be among the target vocabulary or grammar elements if the text is from the course book. Where this is the case, the activity can provide helpful information on how well they are learned.

The salient feature here is making learners aware of **rhyming**, which often appears in poems or song lyrics. The lyrics here have rhyming **couplets**; the last word in the first line of "star" rhymes with the last word in the second line of "are." Likewise, the third and fourth lines end with the same sound /ai/.

Rhyme is a distinctive feature in English for pronouncing sounds that appeal to the ear, and therefore this item should be included at an early stage of learning English sounds. Students will enjoy repeating the lyrics with rhyme, and the rhythmicity makes them easy to learn and remember.

VARIATION
- The lyrics may be unnecessary. The teacher can pause the recording right before, or even after, the target words are played or read for the students to center on them.

007: Bottom-up listening (4/7)
(identifying words replaced with others or mispronounced)

(after assuring that students have understood the passage)
T: I hope you remember the content of the passage we have just done. I am going to read it out loud, but differently from the original. Some words may be changed to other words, pronounced wrongly, or skipped. You have to be all ears, and try to see how many words I read differently.

In the preceding three instances, it is not always necessary for students to turn their attention to the content; the interpretation of meaning may not be involved. This and the following three examples are more content-directed; interpretation of the context is required.

This activity should be given with the course book closed because students will focus solely on listening. It may be performed at the end of a unit or a section. Words to be corrected may be the key words in the context, or the target vocabulary items. If carefully organized, the teacher can assess students' progress in learning particular language items.

VARIATION

- Song lyrics can be used as a fun variation. Students search for words in their worksheets spelled incorrectly or replaced with other words. The level of the chosen materials has to be easier linguistically than that of regular use. Otherwise, students may become frustrated with its recreational nature being placed at risk.

008: Bottom-up listening (5/7)
(finding discrepancies in a picture)

T: (*showing a picture to the class*) Now, take a look at this picture. I am going to explain about it in detail, but some of the explanations will not match what you'll see here. Listen closely and find them.

In this variation of the previous exercise, students concentrate on the content. The teacher asks them to state the number of differences between her descriptions and the picture. For this purpose, materials can be chosen from a course book, a magazine, or a tourist brochure. The image may be put on the board or projected on the screen.

The teacher may also have students improvise descriptions with inaccurate statements and perform her role.

009: Bottom-up listening (6/7)
(listening to the latest world weather in the news)

(*Each student has a worksheet with the world map. At some cities, there are some blanks.*)
T: We are going to hear a weather report from the world news. Listen carefully, and try to catch the current weather

conditions in places on the map with blanks. Fill them in with temperatures and the weather icons: a sun for sunny, a cloud for overcast, an umbrella for rainy, and a cloud with lines for windy. They are clearly mentioned in the recording.

The materials for this activity come from authentic sources of information in media, so it has more relevance to real-life listening skills. Here students' attention is focused on identifying words describing temperatures and other weather conditions. Students need to comprehend the weather vocabulary so that they can answer by drawing corresponding weather icons.

010: Bottom-up listening (7/7)
(listening to plans for the summer)

Students listen to the following recording in which teachers they know—Mr. White and Ms. Brown—discuss their plans for the summer. The students then fill each box in the worksheet below with countries, time period, and people. They are clearly referred to in the dialog.

(the script of a recording)

> Mr. White : I'm going to Europe this summer.
> Ms. Brown : That's great. For how long?
> Mr. White : Two weeks in Italy and a week in Greece.
> Ms. Brown : Oh really? My friend and I are planning to visit Japan and Korea for a week and Taiwan for three days on the way back. Who's going with you?
> Mr. White : My wife. You've met her before, haven't you?
> Ms. Brown : Oh yes, at the Pearsons'.

	WHERE TO	HOW LONG	WITH WHO
Mr. White			
Ms. Brown			

The point is that materials are original to the teacher. The class will be excited to do this activity and learn about the teachers they know and are directly connected with. Students are always curious to know personal information about their teachers. Nothing could be more real-life to learners and nothing could have a better result as a listening skill driver.

Teachers appearing in the recording do not have to be native English speakers. They can be teachers of subjects other than English. The idea is that English is an international medium for communication.

2 Dictation

Dictation can be considered bottom-up listening as it necessitates becoming conscious of individual words. It is rather outmoded, but is still a useful and effective language exercise. A simple format for dictation involves a few sentences with target grammatical structures or vocabulary words, which the teacher may want learners to remember and review.

This exercise can also be used to introduce new grammar, lexical, and especially pronunciation issues. English is referred to as a **non-phonetic language**; the relationship between sound and letter is not strong enough. However, there are rules between them, and dictation provides a good chance to convince students of these rules.

Dictation is effective in teaching other pronunciation features as well that are typically English, such as linking, reduction, and assimilation (see pages 97 to 99). Therefore, the activity can be treated as a unique case of bottom-up listening. The teacher should recognize this distinctive point when practicing dictation.

In practicing this exercise, students may take turns playing the teacher's role and dictating to the class. In this way, they will be responsible for their own learning.

3 Top-down listening

In **top-down listening**, students are more concerned with the overall image of the content than individual sounds or words, or intonation patterns.

011: Top-down listening (1/2)
(rearranging pictures)

Students listen to the following story and arrange the eight pictures in a chronological order.

(*the script of a story*)

Peter arrived to school on foot. He went into the classroom and it was empty. He put some glue on his teacher's chair. His teacher sat on it. Then, she tried to get up, but she couldn't. She was angry and said, "Who put glue on my chair?" Peter replied, "I did." She told Peter to go to the principal's office. Peter reached home late in the afternoon.

(Drawings reproduced with permission and story adapted from Hill, 1980:34)

Students listen to the linear narrative of a story with a clear chronology and arrange the pictures in the correct order. Their attention in this activity centers more on the content than individual sounds or words. For this purpose, the story should be episodically organized and have a story line.

Pictures for use in this activity could be taken from comic strips. The teacher cuts individual panels and shows them on the screen or the board at random. Then, she provides descriptions of the panels, while students determine their correct order.

(Admittedly, listeners may at times refer to individual words, or bottom-up processing. Accordingly, better described as a mixture type this activity may be.)

012: Top-down listening (2/2)
(matching pictures)

Students listen to the following brief conversation and choose one out of the four pictures below where it is likely to take place.

(the script of a dialog)

> A: I would like to exchange some dollars for yen.
> B: Sure, ma'am.
> A: What is the rate now?
> B: We list the current exchange rates on that bulletin over there.
> A: Oh yes, yen has risen.

This scene is likely to take place at a bank. A foreign tourist is visiting the bank to get his foreign currency exchanged. The teacher does not say explicitly, "Now, we are at a bank. The following conversation…" but students can get hints of a probable location from spoken dialog and use them to choose the right picture.

The activity is usable on the condition that students share a common image of where foreign currency can be converted. In other words, they must have a common **schema** involving it. (Schema will be discussed in detail on page 47.) If not, this type of activity would be unworkable.

> **013: Top-down and bottom-up listening combined (1/3)**
> (using recorded materials)
>
> Students listen to a dialog twice from recorded materials. It is a short conversation between two people at a restaurant.
>
> First (for top-down listening):
> Before the first hearing, the teacher asks questions such as below:
> - Where is the conversation taking place?
> - What are they talking about?
> - What is the relationship between the two people?
>
> Second:
> Students listen to the recording and find the answers, and the teacher checks them.
>
> Third:
> Before the second hearing, the students brainstorm words (or phrases) they think they heard during the first hearing.
>
> Fourth (for bottom-up listening):
> During the second hearing, the class are to confirm whether those words actually appear, and correct them if necessary.

Audio materials accompanying a course book lend themselves well to engaging listeners in a chain of top-down and bottom-up listening tasks.

Here in the first step, it takes top-down listening to answer the three board questions. Neither of the two people says, "We are at a restaurant," "We are discussing the budget of our company," nor "I am a salesclerk and you are my boss." All of these are to be inferred from the general gist of the dialog.

During the second hearing, the focus is not on the general picture but on individual words seeking those mentioned in the brainstorming. Therefore, bottom-up listening is required.

VARIATIONS

- As part of top-down listening, a set of multiple choices may be added for the listeners to choose from. For example, the following choices will be given after the question "Where is the conversation taking place?":
  - at a restaurant;
  - at a law court;
  - at the ticket window of a theater;
  - in a classroom.
- As bottom-up listening, the teacher gives the students, before the second hearing,

some detailed questions for concrete or particular information, such as the following:
- What did the two people order from the menu and why?
- What is the total budget for the next month? How much does advertising account for of that budget?
- For how long has the salesclerk been working with the boss?

014: Top-down and bottom-up listening combined (2/3)
(using a real news broadcast)

First (for top-down listening):
Students listen to news items recorded from broadcasts (each of them is only a portion), and arrange the following list in the order that they come out in the recording:
- weather;
- sports;
- natural disaster;
- entertainment;
- economy.

Second (for bottom-up listening):
The students listen to the same recording again to answer more intensive questions, such as these:
- Where will it be stormy and when?
- Which teams played? Which won and what was the score?
- What was the cause of the disaster? How many people are feared dead?
- What is the title of the movie soon coming? When will it be released on video?
- What is the current exchange rate? What triggered the sudden fall?

The materials here are more relevant to students' daily lives and interests. In the first step (for top-down listening), students try to get an overall understanding of what they hear by sifting out relevant information from irrelevancies and redundancies. They also activate the relevant schema in the process.

In the second step (for bottom-up listening), the attention is turned to spotting key words or phrases that provide a clear-cut answer to each question.

💬 VARIATIONS

- As top-down listening, students may listen to one news piece instead of some, and guess what it is about from among the same list.
- As bottom-up listening, students can fill in blanks in a script handout distributed by the teacher with vocabulary words from a given list.

015: Top-down and bottom-up listening combined (3/3)
(using video clips)

The class will watch a video snippet, but before that.

First (for top-down listening):
Students *listen* to the movie dialog *without* viewing the video. While doing this, they try to answer the following questions:
- How many people are participating in the conversation?
- Where is the conversation proceeding?

Second (for bottom-up listening):
Students *listen* to the same portion again while trying to answer another set of questions such as the following:
- Where is the lady sleeping?
- Who is going to pick her at the airport?
- What is the purpose of her visit?

Third:
Students *watch* the relevant portion of the video to confirm their answers.

The first set of questions is for top-down listening, and is concerned with general information or events in the snippet. The second set of questions is for bottom-up listening, and is related to the details of what is explicitly mentioned in the clip.

Videos supply much more information than audio materials. Students can learn background information about where the language is used: the personalities of characters, locations, atmosphere of situations, movements of characters, and other facts. These details are magnified in film, and thus clearly depicted even for casual viewers.

Therefore, as long as film clips used are appropriate for students' proficiency level and interests (and easily accessible), nothing seems more effective and useful as a single teaching material for learners of all ages and all levels.

4 Task listening

Task listening poses two ongoing challenges for students. First, they must understand necessary information given orally, and second, they have to be able to apply the information received to other activities (e.g., clearly discussing, taking notes, outlining), or to other actions (e.g., building a model, drawing a map).

> **016: Task listening (1/2)**
> (picture dictation)

Students make a drawing of their own that they think fits the teacher's description, such as this.

(The teacher reads the following.)

> Draw a two-story house in the center. On one side of the house, there is a tree as high as its rooftop. On the rooftop, a cat is lying face up. On the other side of the house, there is a boy doing something. <u>Freely imagine what he is doing and draw a picture of it</u>.

This activity is a variation on listening to a dictation. The teacher's description has to be simple and clear for any student to draw intelligibly. This activity requires no fixed responses (e.g., the shape and size of the house can be up to each student). Giving some free choice (the underscored portion above) lends color and makes the activity more student-centered or self-expressive. It captures students' imagination and helps them enjoy the process of language learning.

Learners with low motivation to study English but strong drawing ability would fully participate in this activity, which is a positive outcome. The teacher may share the drawings with the class. This bolsters confidence and ensures an increased classroom involvement of such students.

🗨 VARIATION

- Another twist to make the task more entertaining would be to encourage fanciful images in the drawings, such as a turtle doing sit-ups or a talking fish on the magic carpet.

017: Task listening (2/2)
(jigsaw listening)

A group of eight students takes part in the following activity.

First:
The teacher provides each of them with one of the following eight sentences written on eight slips (if there are fewer than eight students, then one of them will be assigned two sentences).

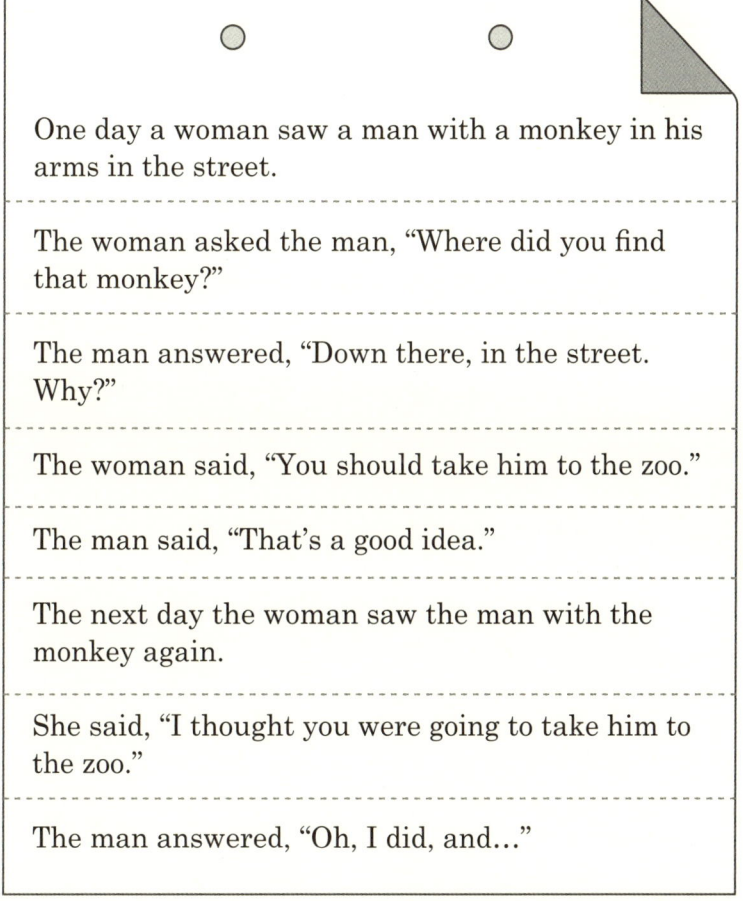

One day a woman saw a man with a monkey in his arms in the street.

The woman asked the man, "Where did you find that monkey?"

The man answered, "Down there, in the street. Why?"

The woman said, "You should take him to the zoo."

The man said, "That's a good idea."

The next day the woman saw the man with the monkey again.

She said, "I thought you were going to take him to the zoo."

The man answered, "Oh, I did, and…"

(Adapted from DeFelice, 2012:43)
(The order of eight sentences above is the original one.)

Second:
Each student memorizes his/her sentence and then gives the slip back to the teacher.

Third:
Students retell the sentences they have memorized to the rest

of the group.

Fourth:
Students discuss and reconstruct in each group the original story by putting the sentences in the correct order.

This activity is called **jigsaw listening**. Students hear different excerpts of a whole dialog and have to exchange information for everyone to share the information necessary to complete the task.

Because the goal is to arrange the order of sentences to reconstruct the original story, students have to carefully listen to the others. Most written materials, whether texts or dialogs, can be used for this purpose.

This activity takes not only listening skills but also contextualizing ability to select the sentences that best fit in the flow of information. If there are two or more groups of eight, they can compete to see which team completes the task first or thereafter compare their results among groups.

What counts is most actual language use involved in the process. What they finally arrive at is not of much account. Similarly, students need not retell the sentences (in the third step above) by using the exact words given by the teacher as long as the content is correctly conveyed.

EXTENSION

- A discussion may follow about how the last line continues after "Oh, I did, and…" In the original, the next statement is "Oh, I did, and he really enjoyed it. Therefore, today I'm going to take him to the movies."

On Speaking

Exchanging ideas through speech is a two-fold challenge for L2 learners. First, words, phrases, and sentences should be combined for the messages to be conveyed. Moreover, certain linguistic skills should be taken to maintain the flow of the conversation. In this chapter, we discuss how to help L2 learners improve their speaking skills from this perspective.

§1 The audio-lingual method

The **audio-lingual method** enjoyed the popularity among language teachers through 1950s to 1960s worldwide. Stemming from Army language training in the 1940s, it was devised to compensate for the shortcomings of **Grammar Translation Method (GTM)**. Disadvantages to the GTM's emphasis on grammar learning and translation are self-explanatory to those interested in training students to speak the target language. The goal of the GTM was to deepen linguistic and academic understanding of the language, not to promote speech.

The audio-lingual method started from the premise that speaking and listening skills are more basic and practical, and these skills can be acquired through the process of habit formation, that is, by repeatedly observing and practicing right models. With this theory in mind, students repeat the model language items (e.g., grammar, vocabulary, sentences) and memorize them so that they become second nature, and therefore this is also known as the mim-mem (short for mimicry-and-memorization) method.

Pattern practice and minimal-pair practice are the two central features of an audio-lingual classroom. **Pattern practice** involves oral drills to practice newly studied grammatical structures. For example, if students have just learned the "There is ..." construction and its meaning, next they would mechanically pronounce sentences using this format following cues from the teacher and repeating the sentences several times. In this way, the class becomes more attentive and orally practices the structure (for details, see page 32).

This practice has the merit of opening up opportunities to learn not only the sentence pattern but also the phonetics of the language in a string of sounds (e.g., phrases and sentences).

Minimal-pair practice is best suited for facilitating discrimination of individual sounds that are difficult for learners to distinguish. The details of this practice are given on pages 85 to 88.

§2 Communicative Language Teaching

Undoubtedly, the audio-lingual method seemed to be what language educators desperately needed, and it remained a dominant method of language learning until the beginning of the 1970s. However, because it placed such an extreme emphasis on repetition and memorization, it was criticized for lack of context, which is always an important factor when language is practically used.

Through pattern practice, which is indispensable in audio-lingualism, students accumulate a structural knowledge of the target language. However, they also need to understand the context, in which the language is used. Critics asserted that language use without context is like learning to drive a car on a simulator. The **audio-lingual method**, when rigorously applied, could produce parrots that constructed perfect sounds, but could not function in actual discourse.

This assertion (together with other theories insisting that language was not acquired through habit formation alone) supported a rationale for various alternate approaches emerging during the 1960s and 1970s. They tried somehow to concern themselves with real-life language use. Those approaches converged on a comprehensive approach known as **Communicative Language Teaching (CLT)**. No doubt, the emergence of CLT was driven by a strong interest in providing skills for successfully handling linguistic challenges in authentic circumstances.

Today, CLT encourages a variety of teaching methods so that students will learn to respond instantly and sensitively to authentic communication, which arises out of sheer necessity, and thus is naturally unpredictable. The necessary skills are improved through interactions and tasks in learner-centered classroom activities.

§3 Communicative competence

Apparently, nowadays there is a common consensus that a successful language learner is synonymous with one with the practical skills required in real-life communication; those skills are commonly known as "**communicative competence**." Evidently, everything in English learning and teaching, from pre- and in-service teacher training to curriculum development, is geared toward producing such language learners.

Communicative competence is a comprehensive term that comprises the following four factors:

- linguistic competence;
- sociolinguistic competence;
- discourse competence;
- strategic competence.

This section will discuss the components mentioned above.

1 Linguistic competence

Let us assume that you are in a train and wish to ask for snippets of information from someone who happens to be sitting beside you. What do you think would happen if you speak only French and they speak only Chinese? Spoken communication would be impossible.

Linguistic competence enables participating speakers to successfully manipulate the linguistic elements of a common language (e.g., grammatical structures, sound systems, vocabulary, and regional or social variation).

2 Sociolinguistic competence

To be a successful and effective communicator, you should not only know the same language but also its correct usage in specific social arenas. The competence to put this knowledge into practice is called **sociolinguistic competence**. For example, if you are invited to a formal party, then you would not probably use the language that is spoken in a relaxed and casual atmosphere of a downtown bar.

Sociolinguistic competence also plays an important role in successful cross-cultural, international communication, where the cultures involved differ in language uses. By some accounts, it totally depends on each culture whether praising the clothes of someone you are talking with is accepted favorably or not. The same is true for asking the first name of someone you are meeting for the first time.

This illustrates how influential sociolinguistic competence is in the context of English as the **lingua franca*** (refer to the footnote) of today's world. All the language teachers need to create recognition of this fact.

3 Discourse competence

Let us examine the following dialog.

---

*lingua franca: a language shared as a means of communication between speakers whose native languages are not the same.

A: It was awful yesterday, wasn't it? It never rains but pours.
B: Is your husband still in the hospital? How is he?
A: Such noise! Didn't get a wink of sleep last night.
B: How long will it be before the doctor discharges him?

The two people in this "dialog" are not communicating with each other. They are just saying what they want to. What is necessary for true communication to take place is **discourse competence** on both sides, or the competence required to keep the conversational flow focused on the subject at hand.

Discourse competence has three components: cohesion, coherence, and conversational discourse. **Cohesion** is a grammatical relationship that links statements and sentences in a meaningful context. A good example is the use of pronouns (underlined).

A: I've changed my glasses. Did you notice?
B: Yes, they look nice on you. Where did you get them?

Coherence is a line of thought or internal logic that combines statements into a meaningful interaction without the help of grammatical linkage. This is illustrated by the following example.

A: That's the telephone. (Will you answer it?)
B: I'm in the bath. (No, I can't.)
A: O.K. (I'll get it.)

(Widdowson, 1978:29)

Although there are no explicit signs of cohesion, the conversation is natural within a meaningful context. Coherence helps the communicators recognize and understand the unuttered statements in the parentheses.

Conversational discourse includes the skills needed to alternately participate in the conversation, that is, the skills to avoid long silences or too much overlapping.

4 Strategic competence

Even smooth and logically flowing communication may stall for some reason. The speaker may suddenly skip to a totally different topic of conversation, or use incomprehensible vocabulary. Something may happen psychologically and the listener's attention may drift off. A fire engine may pass with its siren screaming, drowning out the utterance. A sudden physical action (e.g., sneezing, yawning, or hiccups) may also momentarily break the communication.

When communication stops, interlocutors try to compensate for the breakdown. We call this restoration skill **strategic competence**. It is explicitly and instantly employed when needed; verbally, the following expressions such as "Pardon?", "What do you mean?", "Are you with me?", or "Do you follow me?" may be used.

Of course, you can convey what you wish to say non-verbally as well.

When you realize that the breakdown is your responsibility, you will do something to restore the communication, such as speaking more loudly, clearly, or slowly, or repeating explanations in simpler language, or emphasizing particular part. Each of these linguistic actions constitutes part of strategic competence.

5 The challenge of teaching communicative competence in the classroom

Now that communicative competence has become the center of attention in language learning and teaching, the next problem is how to foster communicative competence in a classroom. This is a huge task because the classroom itself is an artificial and unnatural environment. Communication occurs in a natural, unpredictable flow of changing contexts.

Therefore, thorough preparation is required on the part of the teacher to provide not only authentic or near-authentic settings in the classroom but also a plethora of opportunities to practice communicative skills.

§4 Classroom activities to foster communicative competence

The ultimate goal of teaching speaking is to foster communicative competence. In the activities to develop this competence, learner' attention is directed to the conveyance of meaning without being much conscious of linguistic perfection, which may lead to "tongue-tied."

To reach this aim, however, guidance should be offered gradually from **structure-based** to more real-life **communicative activities**. In this section, we would like to begin with an audio-lingual exercise focusing on how the language sounds at a sentence level.

1 Pattern practice

018: Pattern practice (1/2)
(conventional type)

T: Fill the empty slot on the board with phrases I give you and say it aloud. "Make some coffee." (*Calls on S_1.*)
S_1: "Let me make some coffee."
T: Class, repeat, "Let me make some coffee." (*They repeat it together.*) Next, "Take you to the bank." (*Calls on S_2.*)
S_2: "Let me take you to the bank." Class, "Let me take you to the bank." (*They repeat it together.*)

This illustrates **pattern practice**: a conventional activity in which students fill one empty slot after another with lexical items (words or phrases) provided by the teacher and repeat these sentences after him. Prior to this activity, it is necessary to have learned the target structure and its meaning (in the example above, for the "Let me + bare-infinitive" construction).

This exercise has its advantages: practicing sentence structures and the sounds of English (e.g., intonation, rhythm, modifications). Thus, it should be the first step in learning how to speak. Nevertheless, the problem is clear. It is meaningless, that is, devoid of context and unrelated to students personally. How can we improve it to make it more meaningful?

019: Pattern practice (2/2)
(meaningful type)

T : I am going to give you some cues. Pick one sentence from the board to respond to each of them and say it aloud.
T : "There is something wrong with my bicycle." (*Calls on S₁.*)
S₁ : "Let me fix it."
T : Good. Class, repeat "Let me fix it." (*They repeat it in unison.*) Next, "There has been an accident. Someone's hurt." (*Calls on S₂.*)
S₂ : "Let me call the ambulance."
T : Good. Repeat "Let me call the ambulance." (*They repeat it in unison.*) Then this one, "I'm new in this town."

This is a variation of pattern practice and it is not a repetition exercise. Students need to understand what they see on the board and the hints from the teacher. It can be said that this type of pattern practice is more meaningful than the conventional one. In the second round, only the phrase "Let me" may be erased with students repeating the sentences corresponding the cues.

Variation
- The cues can also be given visually, instead of verbally, by showing drawings or pictures, for example, those of a bicycle and an ambulance in the above exercise.

2 Information gap activities

Communication is most likely to occur in the following two contexts:

- When people want to obtain information from someone who seems to have it;
- When people want to give information to someone who does not have it.

In other words, the prime function of communication is to bridge an information gap between speakers. Various forms of so-called **information gap activities** have been proposed, and they are well-established techniques for teaching students to communicate more naturally even in an artificial classroom setting. Each student works in pairs or in groups, or even in class, and asks to elicit information from their classmates. During the time of this, they negotiate, collaborate, and exchange information to reach a common goal. Students participate in information gap activities feeling more relaxed taking language risks.

This creates a side benefit. By mingling together or circulating around freely, the class feel more comfortable in an otherwise controlled and rigid atmosphere. This may serve as a constructive environment.

020: Information gap activity (1/3)
(collecting information from the peers)

T: We have just learned a type of question: "Did you …?" Now we are going to play a game using it. Here is a worksheet for each one of you.

> S_1 name_____ studied English last night.
> S_2 name_____ watched TV this morning.
> S_3 name_____ went to the library last week.
> S_4 name_____ ate butter and bread this morning.
> S_5 name_____ had a party last week.

T: Everybody, stand up. Walk around and ask, for instance, "Did you study English last night?" according to your sheet. When someone says, "Yes," put his/her name in the blank. You can ask only one question to each person. When you are finished, go back to your seat.

We call this type of information gap activity an **interview game**. Students walk around in the classroom looking for someone who will give affirmative answers, which enables them to review and internalize the "Did you…?" construction in a communicative way. The point is that the information being asked for is personal. This makes the activity more real, even though its purpose is to learn a new target structure.

At the beginning of the exercise, however, the teacher has to ensure that students understand the meanings of lexical items on the worksheet, and remind them of infinitival forms of "went," "ate," and "had." It is a good idea to allow plenty of time to orally practice the questions used in this exercise.

<u>Three tips for communicative activities</u>

Before students participate in communicative activities in pairs or in groups, the teacher must tell them the following:

- How long the task will last. (To encourage students to complete the task)
- What students should do when the task is done, for example, return to their place and sit down. (To stop them from meddling with others)
- What to say when communication breaks down and to repair it, for instance, "Excuse me," "Pardon," "I couldn't catch what you said."

021: Information gap activity (2/3)
(collecting information about the teacher)

(*Each student has the worksheet below.*)
T: What kind of music do you think I like? First, put your idea in the blank after "Your idea" in the worksheet.

What kind of music do you think Mr. Smith likes?*

Your idea: (e.g., Japanese *enka*   )
Ideas of your friends:
  S₁ name_____
  S₂ name_____
  S₃ name_____ } thinks Mr. Smith likes { (   ).
  S₄ name_____   (   ).
  S₅ name_____   (   ).
                                               (   ).
                                               (   ).

(Mr. Smith: teacher's name)

T: Now everyone, ask one another the question in the sheet: *What kind of music do you think Mr. Smith likes?* and get opinions of five persons. Put their names in the underlined sections and their ideas in the following blanks in each line. When you are finished, return to your seat. Let's start.

This is another example of an interview game and may be suitable for more advanced students, who should have learned the "WH-word + do you think + Subject + Verb?" construction. Here they can practice and consolidate their knowledge of this structure in a meaningful way. Prior to this activity, students need to have learned to construct the target structure without difficulty.

The information that is being sought in this exercise is also personal. The point here is that it is about their teacher. Students always become curious to learn about their teachers. They may end up reading aloud their findings and the teacher announcing the actual answers.

EXTENSION
- The teacher can ask the class for input on what they want to know about him, and have them practice likewise on questions made on the input.

Our discussion involves two types of information gap activities so far, both of which are more communicative than mechanical listen-and-repeat drills. Yet, they do not go beyond structural orientation; the first one focusing on "Did you…?" and the second one on "WH-word + do you think + Subject + Verb?"

022: Information gap activity (3/3)
(finding differences between the two)

(*Students are in twos. One of each pair has Picture A and the other has Picture B.*)
T: Don't look at each other's pictures. They look almost alike, but there are five differences between them. Talk about the pictures and find out the five parts in your pictures.

(Picture A)   (Picture B)

This is still another example of an information gap exercise. More advanced students want to involve themselves in more authentic language use, where they can fully activate any and all the language they know. This would be more real than merely practicing the target items.

One of the exercises that meets such a need is finding the differences. This is a popular form of entertainment and hence can be successfully exploited in language classes. By practicing communicative use of the language, students try to find discrepancies in information between the two pictures.

3 Role-play

Role-play occurs in pairs or small groups, and allows students to practice authentic language use in a safe situation. They are less hesitant to talk when hiding behind a fictional character; when they play a role, they might forget being in the classroom, or the presence of their peers or the teacher.

The teacher acts as a facilitator. First, he establishes a scene from daily life (shopping, making a hotel reservation) or a conflict at work, or dialog between child and parent (or even between teacher and student, which will undoubtedly be great fun). Then, the teacher assigns roles for students to act out.

Role-play is performed without much prior preparation by students and a time restriction is needed. The interaction is unpredictable, which is indeed an important factor in authentic communication.

023: Role-play (1/3)
(continuing conversation)

The following conversation ends with Bob saying "Oh...Not yet." Students work in pairs to continue this conversation, with one student playing Mr. Brown and the other Bob. They can say anything quite freely and spontaneously, interacting with each other.

> (*on the first morning at school after a month's holiday*)
> Mr. Brown: Did you enjoy your holiday?
> Bob: Yes, I visited my grandparents. How about you?
> Mr. Brown: We stayed on the farm. Have you finished your homework?
> Bob: Oh...Not yet.

Students work in pairs and interact without any preparation. They are allowed to be as creative and imaginative as they wish in proceeding with the conversation. It can be enjoyable as well as motivating.

Materials used for this type of role-play are easily obtainable; they could come from passages in a course book, for instance. For this activity, the teacher may tell students how many turns should occur between two participants or a time restriction. They would truly enjoy themselves if encouraged to invent something unique, whether real or imagined.

For the second round, partners may be changed with each student keeping the same role as in the first round.

This exercise is very open-ended, and students are eager to know how other pairs work out the forthcoming conversation. Thus, some pairs can be invited to make a presentation in front of the entire class.

024: Role-play (2/3)
(holding imaginary conversations)

First:
Students read the following letter Mark wrote to his mother.

> *Dear Mom,*
>   *Everything is fine. Yesterday, I came to the B&B we were talking about after a week of the hustle and bustle of downtown. What a change! Now I can have some peace and quiet.*
>   *The house actually stands on the hilltop and commands a spectacular view of the surrounding country, even mountains capped with snow and the city lights far beyond.*
>   *I saw the sunset on the horizon in the evening. I even saw the Milky Way at night. I have never seen it in my life before. It was quite an awesome experience.*
>   *Mark*

Second:
Students form pairs.

Third:
One of each pair (S_1) plays the role of Mark who wrote the letter. The other (S_2) plays that of the B&B owner.

Fourth:
The scene is in the dining room on the following morning. Mark and the owner are at the table.

Fifth:
S_1 and S_2, pretending to be Mark and the owner, respectively, start a conversation expected to occur between those two people.

Prior to the role-play, the teacher may have students brainstorm a list of questions the B&B owner might ask Mark during the scene. Alternatively, the teacher could write probable questions on the board.

When S_1 (Mark) has to say something not referred to in the letter, "Mark" is allowed to be creative and say anything to maintain the conversation, which might incur laughter.

For this activity that practices real-life communicative skills, the teacher can use not only a letter but also any type of descriptive materials, such as a travelogue, a diary, or an anecdote. For an anecdote about a historical figure, for instance, one of each pair may play this figure and the partner may play someone s/he wishes to be in a role-play.

VARIATION

- If reading materials are about animals or plants, one student could play the role of one of those and the other could ask questions that can be answered from the context.

025: Role-play (3/3)
(a husband and wife with different opinions)

Students work in pairs. One student in each pair gets Worksheet A and the other Worksheet B. Neither student knows what the other sheet says.

Worksheet A

You are the husband.
You have just bought tickets for a round-the-world cruise for you and your wife. You hope to have a carefree time on the ship. The trip will be your dream come true.

Your Purpose:
To persuade your wife that the trip will be the perfect holiday of a lifetime for both of you.

Worksheet B

You are the wife.
Your husband has brought two tickets for a round-the-world cruise for you and himself. You like boat rides, but do not like the idea of spending several months on a ship. You would rather fly.

Your purpose:
To persuade your husband that it is a waste of time, and that he should cancel the tickets and get air tickets instead.

No matter what the results may be, students will have a good opportunity to practice their speaking skills while responding to the others. If necessary, the teacher may take time to explain or remind students at the beginning about certain relevant language, such as expressions for proposals and denials. Alternatively, these expressions can be given on the role sheets.

For role-play to be more successful, besides scenes and roles, the teacher needs to provide a purpose for negotiating the situation. Students will be engaged in the activity without any problem if they have this background information in mind.

Role-play can include any person, living or dead, real or imaginary.

4 Speeches

Teachers often have students deliver speeches to brush up their communicative skills in a classroom. **Speeches** can be both prepared and spontaneous.

1) Prepared speeches

Topics for **prepared speeches** are determined according to learners' levels, but learners should have some flexibility in their choice of topics.

026: Show and tell

S: Hello, everybody. Have you ever seen something like this? Do you have any idea what it is for? We call it a car cling and we put it inside the car window, not on the outside. That is why letters are printed backwards. It is a free gift I found in a sports magazine. I am going to keep it until I buy a car.

"**Show and tell**" was originally a common classroom activity for young children to develop public speaking skills in English speaking countries. The teacher instructs students to bring to class an item of special significance to them, for example, a souvenir or a gift from a special occasion. Each student shows his/her item to the class and tells a story about it.

Students talk about where they got their items, who they got them from, and other relevant information, including why they chose that particular item. If the item is a picture postcard or photograph of a place they have visited, they can say when and with whom they went and explain the landmarks in the picture.

The speech may be unscripted, although the use of notes is allowed. In case students are not familiar with how to organize their speeches, the teacher should demonstrate it first.

"Show and tell" can be replaced with a speech of a more general kind, especially for more advanced students. The title should be somewhat more open-ended, such as what they want to be, where they want to live, and where they want to visit, along with the reasons for their answers.

EXTENSIONS

- Audiences may work on a personal speech evaluation sheet as shown below. This will help sustain their interest during speeches, and the task can be completed in a short space of time after each speech.
- Listeners can also write down some facts mentioned in the speech, provide a short summary, or frame questions to ask the speaker afterwards, depending on their level of language proficiency.

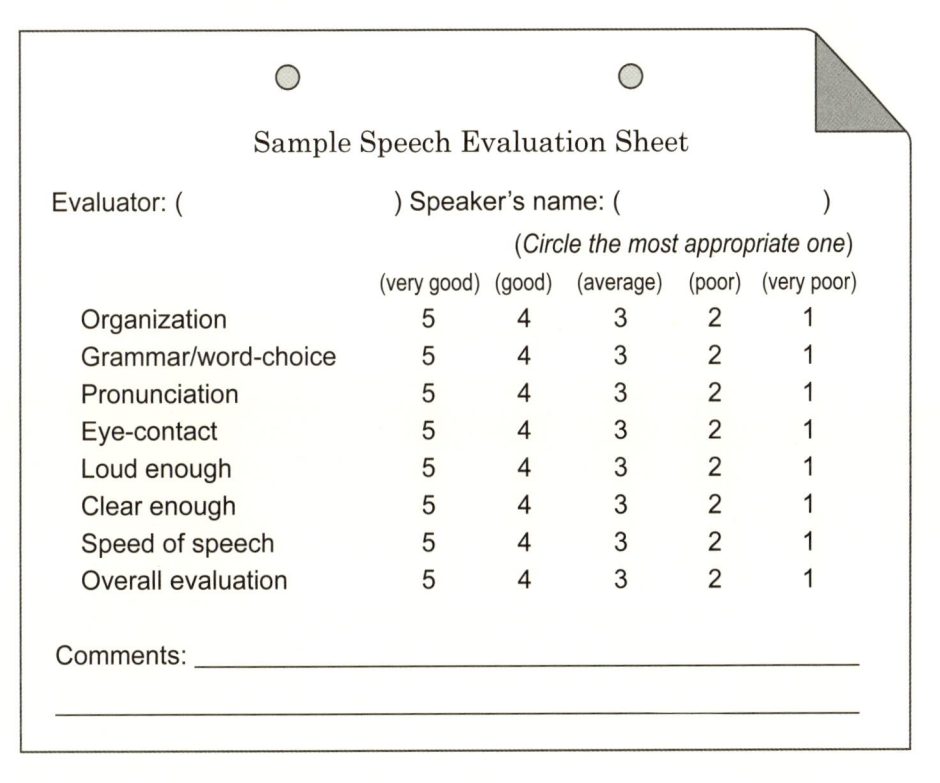

Sample Speech Evaluation Sheet

Evaluator: (   ) Speaker's name: (   )

(*Circle the most appropriate one*)

	(very good)	(good)	(average)	(poor)	(very poor)
Organization	5	4	3	2	1
Grammar/word-choice	5	4	3	2	1
Pronunciation	5	4	3	2	1
Eye-contact	5	4	3	2	1
Loud enough	5	4	3	2	1
Clear enough	5	4	3	2	1
Speed of speech	5	4	3	2	1
Overall evaluation	5	4	3	2	1

Comments: _____

_____

2) Spontaneous speeches

Another type of speech is unplanned or spontaneous in nature. **Spontaneous speeches** are designed to let students practice language use without using notes. Thus, it requires learners to have not only a better command of the language, but also a more adaptable use of it. The teacher may tell them that hesitation markers, for example, *um*, *well*, *kind of*, and *you know*, are not to be relied on too much, but are still quite acceptable.

Delivering a spontaneous speech provides an unrivaled opportunity for learners to acquire skills of self-expression. However, this task is challenging because they have to overcome two psychological hurdles.

One is a concern about having to speak in public without any help, which also occurs in mother-tongue contexts. The second involves learners' doubts about having the linguistic abilities needed to deliver an on-the-spot speech in a second or foreign language.

To alleviate these concerns (at least to some degree), the following two activities may be helpful. In both of these, the teacher acts as a facilitator and timekeeper.

027: Impromptu speech (1/3)
(in pairs sitting behind or in front)

First:
Students split in pairs with someone sitting behind or in front in each line, with one facing back and the other facing front.

Second:
The teacher lists on the blackboard three titles for an impromptu speech, with each one numbered from 1 to 3.

> 1. my favorite music;
> 2. sports I like doing;
> 3. my favorite subject.

(Only students facing front can see them.)

Third:
One student in each pair facing front tells the other student (who cannot see the titles and the numbers) to pick a number from among 1, 2, and 3.

Fourth:
If the student facing back, for example, chooses Number 1, his/her pair gives this student "My favorite music" as an impromptu speech title, and the speech starts.

Fifth:
When the speech is finished, students in each pair change their seats. (Now, those who sat facing back and could not see the board will be able to see the board.)

Sixth:
The teacher writes another set of three titles with each one numbered from 1 to 3. The same procedures of Third and Fourth in the above will be repeated.

Students do most of the talking here. After each pair finishes their speeches, they can start a second round with a different set of speech titles.

VARIATION

- The teacher may provide more choices as a speech title. When students change their seats (in the fifth step above), those choices are retained (instead of replacing them with another set) but with different numbers from the previous practice.

028: Impromptu speech (2/3)
(4/3/2 technique)

Students work in pairs side-by-side. Those who are in the rightmost line will be Student A (S_A), those in the next line will be Student B (S_B), and students in the following lines will be S_A and S_B, alternately.

First:
S_A talks about a topic for *4 minutes* to S_B, who just listens without saying anything. At the end of the 4 minutes, S_A moves one seat back and the student in the back comes to the front to take an empty seat, so that everybody has a new partner.

Second:
S_A again talks to the new partner S_B about the same topic for *3 minutes* this time with S_B just listening. When the time is up, S_A moves one seat back again to get another new partner S_B.

Third:
S_A again talks about the same topic to new partner S_B for *2 minutes* this time and S_B just listens.

After S_A has finished talking about the same topic three times (for 4, 3, and 2 minutes), S_B repeats the same sequence.

The exercise is known as the "**4/3/2 technique.**" Here the teacher's role is to be a director who gives the appropriate directions at every moment.
This technique is useful not only for building oral confidence but also for

developing fluency by speaking on the same topic in multiple times with different partners. The activity is workable in almost all levels of learners. Students can look at the language they have used. Therefore, there should be improvements in appropriate language use (sentence structure, vocabulary, and grammar), speech rate, and redundancy. The number of hesitation markers should decrease as well.

VARIATION

- Instead of the 4/3/2 template, a 3/2/1 or even a 60/45/30 second version seems possible, depending on factors, such as age, linguistic proficiency, students' previous experience.

029: Impromptu speech (3/3)
(talking with a list)

First:
Students are given the following list of question topics. The theme is about food and health.

(Topics to talk about)

Yesterday, what sweets did you eat?
Yesterday, what vegetables did you eat?
Do you ever eat vegetables or fruit for dinner?
Do you ever eat sweets after dinner?
Do you ever read the nutrition labels on food packages?
What food would you eat for a snack, a candy bar or fresh fruit?
What would you choose to drink, regular milk or skim milk?
How likely are you to ask for frozen yogurt instead of ice cream?
Do you ever hear about high fiber cereal?
How likely are you to pick broiled fish instead of broiled beef?

Second:
Students get into pairs and choose at least three topics from the list they want to talk about. If there are no topics of interest to them, they can add what they wish to talk about to the list.

Third:
Each pair starts talking about one topic after another on the list for a limited time.

Fourth:
Discussions end when the time is up.

(Adapted from McCaughey, 2013:51)

The focus here is on improvement of fluency rather than on grammar or correct language usages. Thus, for the activity to be fully effective as it should be, students need to be well informed that they are allowed to do the following:

- keep on talking about one topic;
- move on to another topic (and then onto another one);
- drift off topic as our casual conversations usually do in L1.

The point of this on-the-spot talking is that students engage in informal conversation in a free and easy atmosphere. The list of topics given here is for quick reference in case the discussion slows.

This speaking activity lends itself well to making the material content (for reading or listening comprehension) relevant to students' personal lives. Therefore, the above example is best suited as an activity after studying, or before studying, the material that deals with food and health.

VARIATION
- In the first step above, the teacher can brainstorm with the class possible questions pertaining to a subject from the syllabus or course book.

CHAPTER THREE 3

On Reading

A significant amount of reading of informational texts is conducted in our own native languages every day, but we seldom heave as heavy a sigh as English learners often do in a reading class. Why is this? One big reason is that the way we read in our daily life is quite different from how students read in an English-learning setting. Here an intriguing discussion will take place on how these types of reading differ and what can be done to make L2 reading more similar to L1 reading.

§1 Bottom-up and top-down reading approaches

In this section, the focus will be on what the top-down and bottom-up reading approaches are, wherein the difference lies between them, and how they should be incorporated into day-to-day English-learning circumstances.

1 Grammar Translation Method

In the once well-respected traditional **Grammar Translation Method (GTM)**, a particular concern of students was conducting lexical and grammatical analyses of reading materials and translating them back into their mother tongues to understand the text.

An early prototype of this method stemmed from the European Renaissance of the 14th and 15th centuries, when the written form of Latin, or **Classical Latin** as it is currently known, publically became more easily accessible with the advent of the printing press. People then came to notice striking differences between Classical Latin and so-called **Vulgar Latin**, or the Latin commonly spoken by Roman citizens. Interest in Latin texts, triggered by learning the classical values of the times, led to increased study of the rules of Latin. From this strong inclination for the written form of Latin, a preliminary version of grammar learning and translation emerged.

This method of language learning became well established in universities and schools in Europe during the early 19th century. At that time, higher educational facilities began to open their doors to a wider range of people. Students learned the classical languages, Latin or ancient Greek, as a means of examining the academic achievements of the past centuries in Europe. To study these already extinct languages, it was absolutely necessary to learn the rules of those languages. In this context, the GTM was found to be valuable and had no equivalent.

From the end of the 19th century to nearly the middle of the 20th century, this method, once anchored in schools, was also the primary method used for learning modern languages in many countries. The GTM was a powerful tool for helping students broaden their horizons and knowledge about the world through reading written materials.

Grammar learning requires knowledge of **metalanguage**, which is defined as a specialized vocabulary dealing with the rules of the language (including terms, such as subject, verb, object, complement, adjective, relative pronoun, and modifier). Metalingual knowledge further facilitates discussions of the grammar and structure of a target language, and always goes together with the GTM.

2 The bottom-up reading approach

When students are given written materials to understand through translation, they most expectedly begin with lexical analysis with the help of a dictionary. First, they must try to discern the meanings of each word, then each phrase and clause, followed by each sentence. This reading process is analogous to laying blocks one on top of another higher and higher, and came to be known as **bottom-up reading** approach.

This reading approach is one of the cornerstones of the GTM, and is an important part of language learning—witness its routine use in a place where the major concern is learning how to translate a text to understand it. The students intensively learn and memorize linguistic rules. Thus, the bottom-up approach has its own value and no one can deny this.

However, the bottom-up reading approach places learners at an obvious disadvantage. First, in this approach, readers are too occupied with analysis of the language system to fully direct their attention to what the text has to say. Moreover, reading in this way makes reading rather slow. The whole process inevitably produces bored and apathetic learners because of its inherent difficulty building learner interest and motivation.

In the 1970s, teachers and researchers in English learning and teaching proposed another approach to reading English. This new approach took a cue from L1 reading habits in daily life. What occurs, for instance, when we read a newspaper article? We hardly ever read the text bottom-up with the help of a dictionary.

First, we look at a headline or picture and we guess what the story line will be or create expectations about it. Then, we begin reading.

When this reading style was introduced into L2 reading, it came to be known as the **top-down reading** approach. In the top-down approach, the schema plays an important role.

3 The top-down reading approach and schema theory

A **schema** is a mental image accumulated through social and cultural experiences in our life in relation to, for example, vocabulary words. When we hear the words "the sea," people may think about "fishing and diving," "sunburnt hands," "the icy current," or "a shipwreck." (Naturally, schemas vary by person.) By activating our existing schema, we make a prediction or build expectations about the content, when we set ourselves up to read a text. Schemas also greatly help us comprehend reading materials as we proceed to read.

In an English reading class, readers may sometimes find themselves completely at a loss to interpret a text regardless of their linguistic knowledge. That is mainly because the text lacks the words providing an appropriate schema for readers (or those words do not catch readers' attention).

For instance, let us read the following passage:

> The procedure is actually quite simple. First, you arrange things into different groups depending on the makeup. Of course, one pile may be sufficient depending on how much there is to do. If you have to go somewhere else due to lack of facilities that is the next step, otherwise you are pretty well set. It is important not to overdo any particular endeavor. That is, it is better to do too few things at once than too many... (Cook, 1996:72)

This passage is a perfect example in which linguistic knowledge does not necessarily guarantee a good understanding of the given text. What would occur if you were given the title "About Washing Clothes"? As soon as you see it, you would associate it with your former washing experiences, and your existing schema activates. You would guess that "the makeup" and "facilities" would be "material of fabric" and "a washing machine or dryer," respectively.

Schemas are equally important in L1. One must recognize that a similar situation occurs naturally, particularly in a listening context. Suppose a middle-aged gentleman with no particular interest in clothes happens to be among some fashion conscious young ladies talking about downtown boutiques. He shares the same language with them and hears familiar words in their talk. However, the conversation is intelligible to him simply because he does not have the common schemas those ladies must have in discussing women's apparel.

A marked difference between bottom-up and top-down reading in English learning is that in the former, readers try to grasp the content mainly through knowledge gained from linguistic analyses (e.g., lexical, grammatical, and structural). On the other hand, in the latter, readers depend less on linguistic information and more on activation of schemas to understand the text.

The following activity allows students to activate their schemas and exploit top-down reading processing in reading in an English class.

030: Top-down reading and schema

Students figure out in a short time which one of the four articles matches the headline in the worksheet.

COOL, WET SUMMER FORECAST

1) According to the agency report, humid air will continue to influence the weather up until the end of August, after the official end of the rainy season, bringing the unusual amount of precipitation and unseasonably low temperatures.

2) Four of the 11 cars of the northbound Tulip Express jumped the track just before 9 p.m. No injuries were reported. The tracks run through the city of 23,000 about 120 kilometers southwest of Cosmos. The cause of the accident is being investigated.

3) The paper reports, as of September, 13 % of Diet members were women, about half as many again as in 2000. Among newly employed government officials, who are expected to become the bureaucrats of the future, 35 % of the total comprised women as of late 2013, compared with 30 % in late 2001.

4) A group of 20 airline companies flying from the country's third busiest airport has started discussion on the introduction of the portable detector, the officials said. The low-priced apparatus, made by Cheery&Plum, can instantly shows on a monitor, the atomic numbers of materials inside carry-on baggage.

The headline corresponds with the first article, and solution to this problem calls for the relevant schema to connect the headline with the content of articles rather than a careful linguistic analysis of the text. Readers may only be looking for words describing weather conditions in a particular area. The top-down approach and schema building are therefore like the two wheels of a cart.

💬 VARIATION

- Schemas may be supplied by other than words. A picture, or even sound, can serve the same purpose. The teacher can use those media that depict corresponding articles.

4 Interactive reading

Let us return to the short passage entitled "About Washing Clothes" on page 49. When you know that heading before you read, your schema about washing clothes begins to activate, and you set about reading with a multitude of images and some expectations about the passage. That is typically how the top-down reading approach comes into play.

As you read, you may stumble across ambiguous words, for instance, "make-up" in the second line. It has several meanings, such as cosmetics, an assignment given at school, composition of an object, and quality of a person. Here your schema helps you imagine what it means. You may think, "It is something about clothes; may be the composition of clothes…like type of fabric." In this manner, you make a guess and proceed with your reading looking for clues to confirm whether you have guessed correctly. In this process, your attention focuses on individual words, that is, you shift to bottom-up reading.

This illustrates what usually, and continually, occurs in our daily reading, for example, the reading of a newspaper, a weekly magazine, or directions for how to use a new computer. Thus, besides some extreme cases, we always alternate between top-down and bottom-up reading processing for natural and efficient comprehension. This is known as interactive reading.

If we stick to bottom-up reading, we cannot see the forest for the trees. A serious concern about bottom-up reading in an English class is that if a teacher emphasizes it extensively, students will believe that bottom-up reading is the only option and will not have an opportunity, or even remember, to use a schema even though they may have one. This unusual reading habit is useful only in a few special cases, and therefore an excessive use of bottom-up reading would be the root cause of the stigma of slow and inefficient reading.

Too much emphasis on top-down reading, however, may lead to possible misinterpretation of text, similar to that seen in cases of hasty, careless reading in a native language. From the perspective of L2 language learning, learning about language items (e.g., grammar, vocabulary, sentences) is always essential.

Thus, when reading mainly for content rather than for linguistic analysis, interactive reading is what should be aimed at as a model approach in reading. However, another problem arises here. In what way will it be successfully conducted? That will be discussed in the next chapter.

§2 Three-stage reading activities

Here we discuss in detail how three-stage reading activities could be effectively exploited for reading comprehension by English learners.

1 Background

Whether students are **EFL*** (refer to the footnote) or **ESL*** learners, reading should be at the heart of language learning. In EFL, except for some rare examples perhaps, reading is still a useful device for seeking necessary information given in English. In fact, reading skill has become all the more important as the Internet now offers an effective alternation to other sources of information in our society.

An educational benefit that ESL learners can enjoy in addition to those mentioned above is improving an essential skill to gain access to academic discourse and reach excellence in that context. The rationale for this is the belief that basic literacy instruction should be the cornerstone of public education.

Another tangible benefit to reading is that it helps facilitate vocabulary learning, spelling, and especially writing skills. Reading materials are useful for improving already good models of English writing.

Consequently, the importance of reading cannot be overvalued in language learning. However, students often find themselves feeling dull and lethargic in reading classes. This is possibly because reading is for receiving information rather than giving information, such as speaking and writing, and students become less physically active.

How can teachers encourage them to participate actively in reading classes?

We read frequently and for a variety of purposes in L1, but we rarely moan and groan as learners in an L2 English reading class do. Why is that? Approaching an answer, let us observe at what occurs, before we read, while we are reading, and after we have read in our daily L1 settings.

1) Before we read

We have an obvious reason for reading. For example, we browse through a travel guidebook to gain information about entertainment or

---

*EFL (English as a foreign language): the role of English in countries where it is taught as a subject in schools but not used as a medium of instruction in education nor as a language of communication (e.g., in government, business, or industry) within the country.

*ESL (English as a second language): the role of English for immigrants and other minority groups in English-speaking countries. These people may use their mother tongue at home or among friends, but use English at school and at work (Richard et al. 1993:123-24).

accommodations where we plan to visit.

2) While we are reading
We are actively thinking, saying to ourselves, "The northern part of downtown seems to have less night life. The southern part is far better with lots of fine music venues. Sure it is rather expensive, but the best choice is Bayside Hotel."

3) After we have read
We review pieces of information in a travel guide before making a final decision. We may wish to talk about it with someone we plan to go with. Alternatively, we may refer to another guide if questions are left unanswered.

This is what often occurs before, during, and after our everyday reading, and these steps illustrate a major difference between L1 and L2 reading. Simply, students in English classes do not employ the three-stage strategy as shown above.

It is hoped that this approach helps make reading in an English class operate as in L1 reading, and consequently make reading classes more meaningful and motivating. However, we face a huge challenge in trying to apply that reading strategy to L2 reading because learning in a classroom situation itself is an artificial and unnatural practice. How will it be possible for natural reading to occur in such an make-shift, imaginary setting?

2 Components of the three-stage reading approach

The **three-stage reading approach** in an L2 context contains the following three components: pre-, during- and post-reading activities. At each stage, they are either content- or language-oriented. Whichever activities students perform, the aim is to drive them to read more actively. Next, we discuss in detail each phase with some samples.

1) Pre-reading activities
Pre-reading activities are given before reading a text. Examples and their purposes are as follows.

031: Sample pre-reading activities

Content-oriented
  Students will look at the title or pictures in the text, or lexical items arranged in the order they appear, and do the following:
  • think about a probable ongoing development of the story

if it is a description of an event;
- form an opinion on what seems to be discussed if it treats a social matter.

<u>Language-oriented</u>
Students will do the following:
- study a list of target lexical items from the text with explanations and their meanings;
- look at some sentences where target grammatical structures are used, and guess their meanings and usage from the context.

In pre-reading, content-oriented activities are open-ended and allow students to work in a relaxed atmosphere. They make, confirm, and refute predictions as they proceed with their reading. Alternatively, they research the topic discussed in the text and have some background knowledge.

Purposes:
(content-oriented)
To provide initial impetus and preparation for reading.
(language-oriented)
To have students understand target language items before reading.

2) During-reading activities

During-reading activities are conducted while students are reading a text. Examples and their purposes are as follows.

032: Sample during-reading activities

<u>Content-oriented</u>
Students will do the following:
- draw a picture of a scene from a descriptive passage;
- guess what words or phrases mean within the context, such as seasons of the year, the weather, locations, clothes, emotions, or attitudes of key characters;
- think about why special actions, events, or happenings have come about;
- imagine how the story will develop thereafter, for example, in the following page(s).

<u>Language-oriented</u>
Students will do the following:
- look at a list of target words (with definitions either in

English or in their L1) and identify them in the text;
· think about what or who pronouns (e.g., it, this, he, and she) refer to in the context.

During-reading activities are more varied than the other two types, and they are often placed in either the side or bottom margins in course books.

Purposes:
(content-oriented)
To help hold the interest of learners during reading.
(language-oriented)
To help students with target language items.

3) Post-reading activities

Post-reading activities are given to students after reading a text. Examples and their purposes are as follows.

033: Sample post-reading activities

Content-oriented
Students will do the following:
· freely imagine further story developments after the end;
· form an opinion about the content;
· give their own subtitles.

Language-oriented
Students will do the following:
· compose short sentences using target lexical items (each sentence may logically stand alone or form a coherent passage);
· compose a short sentence using the target grammatical structures.

Post-reading activities allow students more latitude than the two other types. In particular, when the activities are content-oriented, they may work in pairs or in groups to exchange their ideas, and report their discussions to the class. Thus, students can do pieces of work that enable them to practice multiple language skills (see page 103).

Purposes:
(content-oriented)
To check whether students have understood the text and connect the content to their interest.
(language-oriented)

To observe whether students have understood language items correctly and further consolidated their understanding of them.

§3 Rapid reading

The term "**rapid reading**" refers to ways of reading texts more quickly, usually with a certain purpose. This reading approach is intended to overcome a problem that English learners share; they read too slowly. Here we discuss two types of rapid reading: skimming and scanning.

1 Skimming through the paragraph-reading approach

The purpose of **skimming** is to get a general overview of a text rather than specific or detailed information. One skimming skill often implemented in English reading classes is **paragraph reading**.

The paragraph-reading approach is premised on the assumption that once readers become accustomed to the unique discourse patterns of written English, they will quickly grasp the main ideas and relevant information in a text.

The cultural backgrounds of English learners are diverse, for English is more widely used than any other language in the world. To some extent, each culture has its own logical structure, especially in written form. Therefore, when writers present their ideas in English, their responsibility is to make messages easily and correctly understandable to readers of any cultural background. To reflect this concept, writers often develop an extremely reader-friendly writing style. The goal of the paragraph-reading approach is for students to gain familiarity with such a writing style, or logical pattern, and thus be able to read a passage more quickly and efficiently.

Paragraph reading refers to either intra- or inter-paragraph reading. The **intra-paragraph reading** approach teaches students to quickly catch the main gist of a paragraph, and the **inter-paragraph reading** approach teaches them how to grasp the general idea of a passage comprising multiple paragraphs. The following exercises help students become aware of how logic develops in both cases and how these techniques can help them read more skillfully.

1) The intra-paragraph reading approach

What are the functions of sentences in a short passage consisting of one paragraph?

034: Logical development of one paragraph

Students read the paragraph below and consider the roles of each sentence.

> 1) High school teachers have many things to do. 2) They spend a lot of time preparing usually three or four different subjects. 3) During homeroom periods, students come and talk to their teachers about school work. 4) Some teachers also coach a sports team after regular classes, sometimes even on weekends. 5) Other teachers may visit places to arrange field-trips for students. 6) In short, teachers have many duties. 7) But they usually find them worthwhile.

(Okita, 2013:24)

These sentences can be grouped into three sections depending on their functions: a topic sentence, supporting sentences, and concluding sentences.

<u>Topic sentence</u>
The topic sentence summarizes what a paragraph is about and what the writer's point is. The topic sentence in the above is as follows:

> 1) High school teachers have many things to do.

Here readers learn that the passage is about high school teachers, and the writer believes that they have many things to do. In many cases, the topic sentence occurs first in the paragraph, but sometimes it occurs somewhere in the middle or even toward the end of the paragraph.

<u>Supporting sentences</u>
The supporting sentences are intended to provide evidence for the writer's point by giving concrete examples. The supporting sentences in the passage above are these:

> 2) They spend a lot of time preparing three or four different subjects.
> 3) During homeroom periods, students come and talk to their teachers about school work.
> 4) Some teachers also coach a sports team after regular classes, sometimes even on weekends.
> 5) Other teachers may visit places to arrange field-trips for students.

These are descriptions of routine jobs and support the writer's belief about teachers' busy lives.

<u>Concluding sentences</u>
The concluding sentences emphasize the main idea by restating it, quite often with an additional new piece of information. The concluding sentences are as follows:

6) In short, teachers have many duties.
7) But, they usually find them worthwhile.

The writer's opinion is confirmed here, but in different words; "duties" instead of "things to do," as used in the first sentence. This is followed by with extra information. Here, in this case, it is how teachers find their jobs.

That is a typical example of a standard paragraph written in English.

2) The inter-paragraph reading approach
Here is how logic develops in a passage made up of multiple paragraphs and how each of them is related.

035: Logical development of a short passage

Students read the following short passage and observe the functions of each of its four paragraphs.

> New Zealand is one of the countries in the world popular among travelers. The number of people visiting this country is constantly increasing. Last year, I had a good opportunity to visit various places in New Zealand myself, and I seem to have found the reasons for the popularity of the country. This country is really quite safe and full of natural beauty. Let me expand on that.
>
> To appreciate the safety of this country, I only had to be in New Zealand a few days. First, I didn't seem to hear news of violent crimes, like brutal murders or armed robberies, as often as in other countries. They are becoming commonplace in many of the major cities in the world. Next, I didn't feel I had to be careful not to be involved in an unwanted situation, even if I walked alone late at night, say, in downtown Auckland, the biggest city in this country. These two things are enough to tell you how safe this country is.

> Nature seems to be well preserved and protected in this country. Have you ever imagined the ratio of the total area of national parks to the entire area of New Zealand? Parks comprise more than one-third of the land. Moreover, besides national parks, there are many places of scenic beauty, and you don't have to go far from a big city to appreciate the scenery of some of these parks. Only one hour of driving from the hustle and bustle, and you are right in one of them. New Zealand itself is beautiful.
>
> Usually, there are two concerns most travelers have in common. Is it as safe and beautiful as claimed? There seem to be few countries in the world that can answer both at the same time. New Zealand is definitely the first and foremost among these. Besides, you will always find a food court or two in a city shopping district where you can taste unique cuisine from all over the world.

(Okita, 2013:26-27)

The four paragraphs above can be grouped into three major sections depending on their functions: an introductory paragraph, body paragraphs, and a concluding paragraph.

Introductory paragraph

The introductory paragraph, or the first paragraph in the passage above, informs readers of what the passage is about and what the author's opinion is. The passage is about New Zealand, and the author believes that many people are visiting the country for two reasons: its safety and beauty.

The construction of the introductory paragraph is as follows. It starts with a general statement:

> New Zealand is one of the countries in the world popular among travelers.

The paragraph then continues with the author gradually focusing on the points s/he wants to make toward the end of the paragraph:

> This country is really quite safe and full of natural beauty.

Body paragraphs

The body paragraphs, or the second and third paragraphs in the passage above, contain statements supporting the author's perspective from the introductory paragraph.

The author believes that New Zealand is safe and beautiful. The second and third paragraphs support these beliefs about the safety and the beauty, respectively, of the country. Thoughtful readers will be able to predict what the forthcoming two paragraphs will be about when they see at the end of the first paragraph the two key words: "safe" and "natural beauty."

The construction of the body paragraph is interesting. It begins with statements of the paragraph's main point, continues with specific supporting examples, and then ends with reiteration of the main point. This is similar to how single-paragraph passages are constructed, as we have seen in the last section dealing with intra-paragraph reading.

<u>Concluding paragraph</u>
In the concluding paragraph, the author repeats the theme and main points, but in different words from those used in the first paragraph. Quite often, the concluding paragraph ends with an additional piece of information that has not been previously mentioned. In the paragraph above, the new information is about a food court in a big city.

3) Similarities between intra- and inter-paragraph constructions
Similarities between single- and multiple-paragraph structures are crystal clear. The function of the topic sentence in a single-paragraph passage is similar to that of an introductory paragraph in a multiple-paragraph passage. Likewise, supporting sentences in a single-paragraph passage are akin to supporting paragraphs of a longer structure, and the concluding sentence is similar to the concluding paragraph.

Here we focus on the paragraph-reading approach as a method of skimming through a text. The linear nature of the logical structure mentioned above is a typical example of what constitutes a paragraph written in English. However, paragraph reading is not suitable for use with passages of fictional prose or narratives with less conventional structures.

2 Scanning

For rapid reading, skimming is intended to hold a bird's eye view of the text. The purpose of **scanning**, however, is quite different. The following task helps students understand where scanning can be usefully employed.

036: Scanning

Students examine the TV schedule below and answer the questions that follow.

Ch/time	6:00 pm	6:30	7:00	7:30
1	GBA Basketball: Brooms vs. Dustpans (5:30)			
3	Fight Forward!	Mama Knows Best	Movie: The Old Man and the Sea	
4	College Football: Fighters vs. Gangsters			
5	USA This Week		Wheelie the Horse	
7	Asian Cuisine	Kawach Folk Dance	Rambus the Great	Animal Kingdom
9	Movie: Auckland Connection			Business Today
12	Cartoon: Dorae Mon	Asian News	Larry Queen	
15	X-Team	Fauna and Flora	Green Thumbs	
21	News Flash	Movie: The Prince and I		

- How long does the GBA Basketball game last?
- What time does "Wheelie the Horse" come on?
- What channel is showing "Larry Queen"?
- What movie starts on Channel 3 at 7:00?
- What show comes on after "X-Team" on the same channel?

For this exercise, readers do not need or want to know everything about the programs. All they need are a few pieces of reliable information concerning the times, channels, and names of specific programs. There could be no better setting for scanning than this; we scan for some particular and exact information.

VARIATION

- A myriad materials are readily available for the exercise, for example, train schedules, information maps, advertisements, telephone books, and pamphlets for travelers. They are a treasure trove of materials for scanning.

3 Differences between skimming and scanning

Three prominent differences should be highlighted between skimming and scanning.

The first and most important is that skimming is for general information, while scanning is for specific information.

Second, skimming should be used when readers have no previous information about the content or structure of what they are reading. Scanning, on the other hand, is best used when readers know beforehand not only what information is contained in a document but also how it is presented. For example, when we wish to know a telephone number, we pick up the directory because we know what information it provides. In addition, we know how numbers are listed; they are organized by number holder name in alphabetical order. This is also true when we want to know when and on which station a live telecast of a soccer game begins. We know which page to turn to in the newspaper and how the necessary information is arranged on that page.

Finally, the information being sought through skimming does not have to be exact. This is not true for scanning, which lends itself well to identifying specific information.

It is worth remembering, however, that apart from some extreme cases, scanning and skimming generally occur not in isolation, but alternately and interdependently during the day-to-day reading process.

CHAPTER FOUR

On Writing

A problem with L2 writing is that it has traditionally been treated as an extension of linguistic structure instruction. This long-standing practice has made writing exercises lose their original purpose of teaching students how to convey written information to their audience.

Before the above problem is addressed, it is necessary to clarify a difference and similarity between L1 and L2 writing. The difference is that writing in L2 acts as a springboard for the application of newly learned language forms and vocabulary to speaking activities, while this is not true for L1 writing. The similarity with its nature is that writing has to be practiced routinely and systematically, much the same as a musical instrument and sports have to.

With this foregoing discussion in mind, this chapter provides some helpful insights into teaching L2 writing skills.

§1 From composition to communicative writing

Until the early to mid-1980s, L2 English classes emphasizing production ability in writing were titled "English composition," or the term "composition" appeared elsewhere in syllabus descriptions. However, the word "writing" has recently replaced "composition" in course title names. What is the rationale behind this? The question initiates our discussion of today's wider trend in writing classes.

1 Composition or writing?

For many years, a major concern of English teaching has been teaching about the language (e.g., grammar, vocabulary, and sentences). English writing activities were exploited to facilitate learning of those language items. That was particularly true where grammar learning and translation were firmly established as a basic premise of language teaching. The writing classwork done in such contexts was often called composition.

A typical example of "composition" is a teacher presenting a new linguistic concept, then providing a sentence in the students' mother tongue to translate into English by using that concept. This is a typical process of "composition," or creating something by joining parts of elements. The teacher then examines the translation and evaluates how accurately the target structures are used. In this sense, composition is teacher-directed.

However, this approach to writing is rather separate from the nature of writing. Writing occurs when we have information we seek to impart to an interlocutor. We write e-mails or snail letters to our friends (or even to someone we have not met before) to say what we have to say. Another example is creating a report or thesis for academic purposes. Whatever the reasons or situations may be, writers have a message to get across to someone they want to read it.

Accordingly, it is quite natural even in an L2 context to consider writing a medium for passing on information rather than for learning about language. The new communication-focused approach to writing instruction is known as "communicative writing" or just "writing." The writing activities given in this setting are generally student-directed.

2 Criteria for accessing writing assignments

Even for native speakers, it is a daunting task to present one's ideas in writing with correct language usage and logical discourse. It is still more demanding for students whose native language is not English. To acquaint non-native English learners with accurate skills, a teacher with a sense of purpose can take advantage of a broad spectrum of writing activities.

On one end of the spectrum is teacher-directed writing, in which students write down model sentences shown by the teacher. The practice is mechanically done with attention on form, or whether language items are correctly and neatly copied. There are no choices extended to learners. This exercise is closed-ended and allows only one possible response from them.

On the opposite end is student-directed writing, which enables students to decide almost everything about their work: what to write about, how to write it, and whom to write to. In this case, the attention centers on what the language means, or whether messages are successfully transmitted to the interlocutor. The teacher's responsibility is not to control but to facilitate the process. It is generally open-ended, and various responses are expected from the writers.

Next, we examine some sample writing practices across the spectrum, starting from teacher-directed exercises to student-directed.

3 From teacher-directed to student-directed writing

037: Copying sentences down from the board

Students copy the following sentences written on the board.

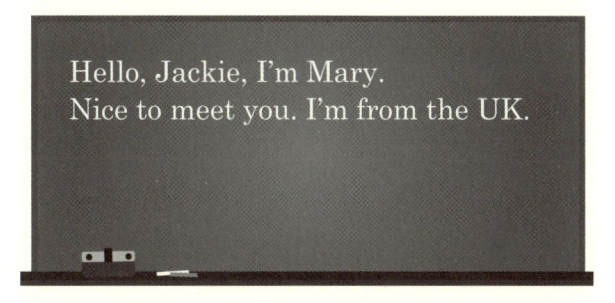

> Hello, Jackie, I'm Mary.
> Nice to meet you. I'm from the UK.

The model sentences here may come from a course book. This is an extreme example of a teacher-directed writing activity. Students concentrate on the form of the language; correctness is all that counts. This method runs counter to a present trend toward communicative language learning and teaching.

However, we cannot reject practices such as this out of hand. Indeed, they need to be the center of writing during the earliest stages of English learning, particularly for learners whose mother tongue is not based on the Roman script. These learners have to work out a completely new writing system. The activity above thus offers them an obvious advantage. An underlying idea behind this exercise is that practice makes perfect.

EXTENSION
- Another challenge could be added by a student-directed touch. Students can replace the words "Jackie," "Mary," and "the UK" with whatever they like, real or imaginary, such as "Hello, Mickey Mouse. I'm Moominpappa. Nice to meet you. I'm from Finland."

038: Arranging and rewriting words

Students arrange the words in each pair of parentheses shown on the board, so that the version will bear a personal relevance.

> (woke / at / six / I / up).
> (then / I / seven / at / home / left).
> (to / school / saw / Miss White / I / on / my way).
> (she / English / our / teacher / is / new).

Here structure is the focal point. Students first have to correctly arrange the sentence parts into sentences. However, they have more leeway in this activity than in the previous one. They create new versions of these sentences about themselves. This part of the exercise allows a wide variety of responses from them.

This is a good example that students even at a primary level can enjoy writing something meaningful by making use of a simple template. Inviting them to write about themselves is an effective way to make writing practice more inspiring and motivating than just arranging words.

039: Changing words to match a picture

Every student has a handout of the following short passage and drawing. They then rewrite the passage in their own words to make it corresponding to the drawing.

> At the park, a young man is sitting on a bench. He is reading a newspaper. It is snowy.

It can be clear that this activity is teacher-directed because the teacher prepares the original passage and drawing. However, it is simultaneously student-directed because learners can decide how to rewrite the given sentences. That is, they can choose which words to replace with words from their own vocabulary inventory.

"On a bench" could be replaced with "on the grass," "by the tree," "beside the flowers," or "under the sky." Similarly, "a newspaper" can become "a magazine," "a comic book," "a novel," or even "an anthology," and "It is snowy" can be changed to "It is sunny," "It is bright and clear," or "It is a beautiful day."

Sometimes, words chosen to replace the original ones may be unsuitable or incorrect. If this occurs and those words have surface-level grammar or spelling mistakes, it is important to recognize that part of the aim of such practices is to encourage students to learn to write independently in a low-stress environment, which is not the case when the focus is on learning of correct forms of language use. Linguistic perfection should not be pursued here.

Drawings or pictures for use in this activity are easily obtainable from the course book as well as from magazines and other resources.

EXTENSION

- Students can freely describe what the drawing suggests the person in it feels, hears, or smells. For example, "He feels warm and comfortable," "He hears birds singing," or "Something smells sweet."

040: Imaginary writing

Students rewrite the underlined parts of the following in-flight announcement and create their own versions. The teacher tells the class that the plane can fly to anywhere, even to the future or past, at any speed, and that their ideas can be as crazy and funny as they like.

> Welcome aboard <u>flight 210 to Los Angeles</u>. Our flight time will be <u>about 10 hours</u>. Please <u>put your bags in the compartments above your seat or under the seat in front of you</u>. After <u>dinner</u>, we will <u>show you two movies</u>. Thank you and enjoy your flight.

(Adapted from Tachibana, 2014:20)

This example is similar to the last one because students can rewrite a given passage in a relaxed atmosphere while directing attention to content rather than form.

The difference, however, appears to be that the activity here stimulates students' creativity more than just changing words to match the picture. This is because the use of a picture or drawing is in fact prone to make their imagination less active, thought visual materials themselves are an appealing and effective teaching aid.

Another apparent benefit here is that the teacher will be pleasantly surprised by the students' creative power. This would be unlikely to occur in form-focused writing. The responses are naturally limited and the teacher often finds himself in the drudgery of checking their writing for linguistic mistakes, such as spelling and construction.

Materials for this type of exercise are easily available in a course book, and even a weak student can enjoy participating in it.

Extension

- After the announcements are completed, the teacher can display them on the notice board for everyone to appreciate. In this way, they would be given impetus for another writing activity of a similar type.

041: Constructing short sentences

Students pick three lexical items from the following list of five written on the board and make three short sentences. There is no need to connect the sentences in context. They can stand alone.

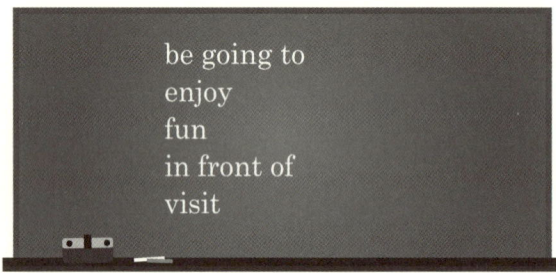

```
be going to
enjoy
fun
in front of
visit
```

One clear reason for having students pick three out of five is to give them room for free choice. When learners have gained a basic knowledge of the grammar, structure, and vocabulary needed for writing, they can further proceed to activities such as this.

The purpose of this writing is for target words to become part of students' **active vocabulary*** (refer to the footnote) and be reinforced for their future use. Therefore, the exercise can be conducted at the end of a unit or a section in the course book. The suggestion is that target language items are best consolidated in context.

---

*Active vocabulary: the words that learners use when writing or speaking. The term is used in contrast with **passive vocabulary**: the words that learners understand when seeing or hearing but don't use.

EXTENSIONS

- To make the activity more challenging, the teacher can tell students to connect the sentences logically.
- The teacher can tell them to make those sentences reflecting their own experiences. Purposeful is synonymous with student-directed, and writing will be more successful when it is personally relevant to writers.

042: Dicto-comp (1/2)
(traditional type)

First:
Students look at the following words on the board.

> Tom – hiking
> friend's house – bus – harbor
> ferry – island
> walking – trees

Second:
Students listen to the following story without taking notes.

(*The teacher reads the following.*)

> Tom decided to spend the day hiking on the island. He went to his friend's house and they took a bus to the harbor. There, they got on a ferry and soon they reached the island. After a few minutes, they were walking among beautiful trees full of red blossoms.

Third:
Students then write a new version of the story, using those words on the board. They can use words of their own to reconstruct their stories.

This activity is called "**dicto-comp**," or "**dicto-gloss**," and it marries dictation and composition. Here students first engage in active listening, and then produce their own versions of the story using the given words. However, their stories do not need to be identical to the original. One possible example can start with the following:

"Tom wanted to go hiking with his friend. They went to the harbor by bus..."

This exercise leaves learners more scope for language manipulation, which is not the case for dictation.

Another difference between dictation and dicto-comp is that although they both involve listening, **dictation** requires **bottom-up listening**, while dicto-comp is apt to require **top-down listening**. That is, dictation aims at individual words and other linguistic features (e.g., linking and reduced forms), while dicto-comp concentrates on receiving the heart of the message.

VARIATION

- Without the benefit of the words on the boards, students listen to the story and jot down key words depicting a general idea of the passage rather than the details. They then reconstruct the story using those key words.

043: Dicto-comp (2/2)
(interactive type)

T : Today, we are going to write about Australia. (*Writes on the board "Australia" at the top.*) Where is the country? Any idea?
S_1: It is in the Pacific Ocean.
T : Yes, it is in the southwest Pacific Ocean. (*Writes on the board "the southwest Pacific Ocean."*) What else do you know about the country?
S_2: Sydney, big city.
T : Good. Sydney is the country's largest city. (*Writes "Sydney."*) What else?
S_3: Opera House is in Sydney.
T : Yes, the Opera House is a famous building there, the landmark of the city, so to speak. And, many tourists visit the place. (*Adds to the list "the Opera House" and "tourists."*) Does anybody know the name of the people living there from the earliest times?
S_4: Abo...something.
T : Right. Aboriginals. (*Further, writes "Aboriginals."*) Now, class, look at the blackboard. Let's look back what we talked about Australia and you are going to write about it. When you write, please use the words on the board.

> Australia
> the southwest Pacific Ocean
> Sydney
> the Opera House
> tourists
> Aboriginals

This is a variation on dicto-comp. In this activity, words are elicited from learners through student-teacher interaction, which is a defining feature of this example. Here they are highly motivated because they chose the target words themselves. Students will be more interested in the exercise if corresponding pictures are also presented as visual aids.

044: Predicting the development of a passage

Students read the following passage from a course book and think about how the story will develop after it ends.

> One evening, I was taking my dog for a walk around the block, when suddenly I saw a faint flashing light in the northern sky. As I was watching it…

Considering probable further developments of the passage, students need to read between the lines. In this example, reading has a much larger focus than in any other activity so far. The materials for this use should have a logical structure and strong story line.

To put a message into written form, learners need to employ all their knowledge to write plainly, intelligibly, and logically. This activity is appropriate for those with advanced writing skills in not only grammar and vocabulary but also in discourse and paragraph construction. Therefore, the exercises of this type could be a final step leading learners toward student-directed free writing.

The above assignment is extremely open-ended, and students, once accustomed to it, will enjoy thinking up creative and imaginative solutions.

VARIATIONS

- The teacher can show a passage from the course book with the middle part omitted. Students can then freely imagine what may have been identified in the

missing portion and write it out.
- The teacher can use any dialog from a course book with the ending left off. When it is between two people, the possible ending lines will be worked out in pairs and enacted in a role-play.

045: Filling in an empty cartoon "bubble"

Students freely imagine and write down a statement that could go inside an empty speech bubble in the worksheet.

This activity leaves more room for students to stretch their imagination. If they are told that the outcome is open-ended and linguistic perfection is not necessarily required (even L1 vocabulary may be partly used), then their anxiety is alleviated and a varied range of responses can be expected. This will be extremely enjoyable and challenging.

Inevitably, students feel inspired to present their writing in class and simultaneously curious to know what others have written. Nothing could be a better case than this where the teacher can apply a multi-skill approach (writing, oral presentation, listening to peers' presentations, and reading to confirm their content later provided in written form) (see page 101).

If there are vocabulary words or structures that need to be reviewed or reinforced, they may be usable in this writing work.

VARIATION

- Picture books provide another attractive source of material for this activity. Each page is handsomely illustrated with brief lines. The teacher can display a page on the screen with the lines covered up. He then has students re-create those lines.

046: Writing haikus

Students write haikus and describe a general or universal human feeling, idea, or concept, such as natural beauty, justice, or life itself. They later share their haikus.

A **haiku** was originally a simple form of Japanese poetry containing a season word and composed of three lines of words (five, seven, and five syllables per line from the top). The lines do not rhyme. Each season word indicates its particular season in which the haiku is set. For example, snow flurries can represent winter. Therefore, its genius is using the smallest number of words to describe the depth of natural beauty and human feelings we experience in our daily lives.

Claiming poetic license, this activity can be flexible. English haikus need not follow the strict syllable count, nor do they require the use of a season word. Haikus are not too demanding to write, and students avail themselves of unique opportunities to directly and openly express themselves with the vocabularies of their choices.

Writing a haiku is also one of the few student-directed assignments that learners at all levels of linguistic knowledge can do. Haikus also amuse audiences; the readers assess its quality.

Here are two examples:

>   in the autumn dusk
>   the parrot repeats the name
>   of its dead master
>
>   (Sakamoto, 1996:75)
>
>   house for sale---
>   the apricot tree in bloom
>   as never before
>
>   (Yoshimura and Abe, 2003:72)

047: Journal writing

Students write about their daily lives and submit their writing at the beginning of each week or month. The teacher returns it with comments.

The word journal comes from the Latin *diurnal*, or daily. In its journey through French and into English, the word came to mean "diary." In **journal writing**, which is quite often seen L1 class, students are not unduly concerned about making mistakes (or even jotting down garbled language.) This lenient approach is critical to the improvement of better writing skills, and is just as valuable in L2 class as in L1 class.

Whether it is in L1 or L2, the premise is that writing should take time and effort, and be done "little and often" without constraints, and its skill can be improved only through writing, similar to how speaking skills can only be improved through speaking.

The teacher reacts to the writings with comments, opinions, or advice, thus adding an authentic, meaningful dimension to this and motivating students to engage in additional writing.

A potential benefit of this task is lowering the psychological barriers students bring to the classroom and opening up an avenue for building good rapport with their teacher. Conversational replies (e.g., "You are really sad, aren't you? I hope your dog will be back before long.") may be included in the comments.

Students enjoy this activity regardless of their level. They do not need to worry about the number of words and can work at their leisure.

048: Writing to a host family

Students are going to visit Canada on a home-stay program. They are writing to their host families, seeking information about what things are like in and around the area prior to their visit.

This assignment is highly meaningful to students because in this context there is someone to write to personally for practical advice.

With English being established as a global **lingua franca**, opportunities to write to international audiences have been increasing. When learners write English in such settings, they may face the additional challenge of having to be sensitive to the people from diverse cultural backgrounds. Therefore, this activity leaves some room for the teacher's guidance. Students need to be reminded how to write in a reader-friendly and culturally unbiased manner. The language teacher will play a prominent role as a cultural mediator in this context.

§2 Authenticity

In the previous section, we examined writing activities from both teacher- and student-directed perspectives. Along with these criteria, there is another criterion for evaluating writing activities: their inauthentic or authentic natures.

Inauthentic classwork is designed only for use in ESL or EFL classes, and thus lacking real-life relevance. For instance, a teacher may ask students to arrange random words in the correct order. Such exercises serve only for testing or reinforcing the understanding of target language forms and vocabulary. Those activities would never be conducted in real life, much less in a native language situation.

Authentic classwork, on the other hand, is related to writers' real lives. They may have a practical purpose, which can probably be applicable in real life. Journal writing in L2 learning is a case in point. The same task may be given in L1 writing as well.

The following is another good example of an authentic activity.

049: Completing an application form

(Each student has the following application form.)

T : Let us suppose that you are applying for an overseas language program. Now, fill out your form. In writing your reasons of application, be sure to write something persuasive. Please print clearly.

APPLICATION FROM

Name(LAST, First):
RESIDENCE:
PHONE:
BIRTH OF DATE(Day, Month, Year):
AGE:
EDUCATION(Admission Month/Year, Name of School,City,Country):

INTERNATIONAL EXPERIENCE:
INTERESTS:
REASONS OF APPLICATION:

This activity is authentic because it is common practice to fill out application forms. For this type of practice, students can write a resume for their on-coming possible job searches, or complete forms and cards of any type in real life, such as for a hotel reservation, a customs declaration, or a market questionnaire.

EXTENSION
- This activity can be easily converted into a multi-skill language task (see page 107).

§3 The process and product approaches

In this section, the process approach is observed with sample classroom activities. In what way does it differ from the conventional approach to writing instruction?

1 The process approach in contrast to product approach

Normally, in an ESL or EFL writing course, the teacher gives students a general subject or two to write about. They then narrow down the subjects and choose a related topic. Some students may think about preparing a draft without actually knowing how. Some may finish it sooner and look over their writing before submitting, without knowing how to improve it. Some may not manage to finish it in time and will need to take it home to complete.

The teacher collects finished papers for review. He carefully examines and evaluates them based on the correctness of forms, or on how correctly target language items, if any, are applied. He may make corrections, and then returns the papers for students to correct for the final versions with some comments on the content.

That is a basic outline of the so-called **product approach**, the term used here for conventional writing approach.

In contrast, the **process approach** takes a cue from what we do in L1 writing. Every one of us can remember practicing writing at school. We begin by deciding on a topic, assemble our beliefs or views, and proceed with our writing. Along the way, we may ask for advice, and when we have finished a first draft, we check it for possible mistakes, ambiguity or redundancy. The entire procedure concludes when we confirm that we have successfully conveyed our message.

The process approach starts from the premises that follow:

- Writing skill is polished by practicing writing rather than the teacher correcting linguistic errors or mistakes.
- Writing should be a voluntary action and be connected with a setting that leads learners to the development of **learner autonomy*** (refer to the footnote).
- Guidance should be given from the perspective of its audience: on how to write in a reader-friendly, persuasive, and impressive manner.

The teacher's role in the process approach is not to judge or supervise, but to serve as a mentor or coach to help students through the writing process before the final outcome is reached successfully.

2 Three components of process approach

Process writing involves three phases: getting started, preparing a draft, and proofreading.

1) Getting started

If the teacher gives students a broad subject to write about and no other guidance on the writing process, they may be confused about where and how to get started. Thus, in this phase, the teacher helps students prepare to write.

Getting started is comprised of four cookbook steps: listing, brainstorming, quick writing, and mapping. Each one of these is illustrated below.

---

*learner autonomy: a student's ability to establish realistic goals and take responsibility of his/her own learning.

Listing

050: Process approach>getting started>listing

T : We are going to write about our school life. First, list any word or phrase that springs to mind when you think about it. You may wonder if some on your list fall under the theme, but don't worry about it. Keep on drawing up the list.
(after assuring that the job is done)
T : Okay, please check your list from the top down. If you think some of them do not fall under the subject, you can cross them off.

The first in a sequence of the four is **listing**. It is individual work, and its purpose is to help narrow down the general subject *Our school life*, and select a specific topic. The point of this activity is to keep students open-minded, without concerns or inhibitions in trying to decide on the topic. They just jot down all the free associations triggered by the subject, and may hit on a new or unique idea they have not previously considered.

Brainstorming

051: Process approach>getting started>brainstorming

T : Now, let's form some groups of four. In each group, all of you will take turns and read out your lists aloud. During that time, other students take a look at your lists and listen carefully. If someone says any item not on your list, you can add that item to it.
(after some time)
T : Have you added any item to your list? Now, choose one from among your list you want to write about. That will be your topic.

Brainstorming is creative group work and a well-established technique designed to generate ideas from students in an informal discussion. It can be conducted with a larger group, such as an entire class, unless students feel uncomfortable speaking out. Positive feedback from the teacher can be expected about contributing freely to the discussion, as there are no "correct" or "incorrect" ideas.

The aim is to come up with as many ideas as possible about the subject without tight constraints, and then review the practicality of the ideas afterward.

The initial subject given by the teacher is wide-ranging. This activity helps students develop a more concrete or specific idea of what to write about, and leads them to decide on their topics.

Quick writing

052: Process approach>getting started>quick writing

T : Have you made your mind which topic to write about? Take another sheet of paper. Write the name of your topic on top. Next, write down any words or phrases you think of under that title. Just keep writing without stopping and without worrying too much about spelling. You could even write, "Can't think of any" if nothing ever crosses your mind. Just try to keep on writing.

Quick writing is also called **free writing** or **wet ink**. The teacher should emphasize the importance of "not worrying too much about spelling." Otherwise, students would pay too much attention to spelling issues, and feel hindered from concentrating fully on the task.

At the outset, the teacher may say, "Write down at least 20 items," with the forthcoming activity in view.

Mapping

053: Process approach>getting started>mapping

T : I suppose each of you has a list of words or phrases. Now pick some items that you think are more linked with your topic than the others, and narrow your list down to 10 to 15.
(*after some time*)
T : Take another sheet of paper. Write the title of your topic in the center and put a square around it. Now, divide your list into some groups. Items in the same group have something in common. There may be an item seemingly having nothing in common with another. Then, that single word or phrase forms one group.
(*after some time*)
T : Have you put them all into some groups? Next, put each group around the title of your topic and link them with lines.

Mapping concludes this phase of getting started.

Successful writing takes competent organizing skills. In mapping, students draw a graphic representation of key words or phrases. The mapping is intended to help organize ideas in a logical manner.

If the topic chosen is "club activities" and words or phrases from quick writing are, for example, "after school," "basketball," "badminton," "chorus," "gardening," "gym," "on weekends," "quilting," "school paper," "soccer," "sports field," and "track-and-field," then the mapping will resemble the following diagram:

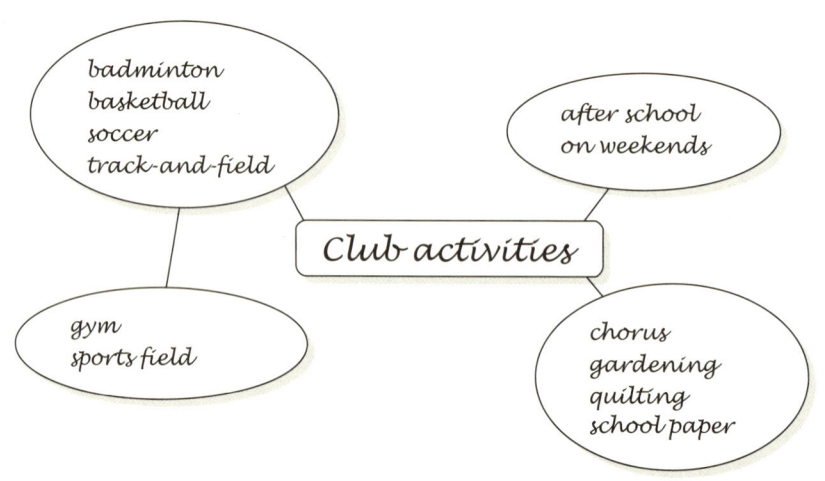

badminton, basketball, soccer, track-and-field — *after school, on weekends* — **Club activities** — *gym, sports field* — *chorus, gardening, quilting, school paper*

A sample of mapping

2) Preparing a draft

Once the topic has been decided and key words or phrases to be used have been provided, students can start preparing a draft. However, before that, the teacher may convince them of the importance of writing in a reader-friendly manner. In other words, careful reflection is needed on how to organize a paragraph, how to develop a written discourse, or how to write persuasively and effectively by exploiting rhetoric. Here the diagram of mapping from the previous activity serves as a chart.

3) Proofreading

A notable feature of the process approach is this proofreading phase. Students here get some suggestions for improvement from their classmates. This is known as "peer editing."

054: Process approach>proofreading

T : Now, you have finished the draft. Next, let's make some
　　pairs. Read your partner's draft and write down your
　　comments or suggestions for improvement in the margin

according to "Points to note" on the board.

> Points to note
> 1. Is the draft reader-friendly?
> 2. If not, what is your suggestion for improvement?
> 3. Does each paragraph keep to one topic?
> 4. Is the draft persuasive?
> 5. If not, what is your suggestion?

By **peer editing**, students not only get suggestions for improvement from their friends but also are encouraged to read their writing actively and critically. This leads them to assess their own drafts more objectively for the final review. Moreover, they get to know each other through this activity and establish a good rapport. This alone would be enough to make the task a valuable opportunity for them.

Any comments from students should be given in writing, not orally. Given orally, it should make the teacher difficult to evaluate them, when necessary. When drafts are returned, students reflect on those comments and revise their drafts if they think it is required. When the revisions are completed, new and final versions are submitted to the teacher, who reads and returns them with some feedback.

Feedback from the teacher, as well as peer editing, makes the process approach unique. It is also important how the teacher responds to mistakes or errors. He should be very careful not to make corrections in red, as is often the practice with the conventional product approach. Primarily, mistakes or errors should be corrected by students themselves. The teacher's role is to open up opportunities for them to improve their work rather than to identify the flaws, which are naturally and usefully being made in honing writing skills.

CHAPTER FIVE

On Pronunciation

English is generally regarded as the dominant language of communication in the international arena. This makes it all the more important for English students to learn speaking with standardized pronunciation. If we have a round-table discussion in English among individuals with different L1 backgrounds, for communication to be facilitated, participants will need to speak without much variation in pronunciation.

§1 General American English and Received Pronunciation

It is true that English learners should not place any value judgments on advantages of learning one type of English over another. Nevertheless, the country with the largest number of native speakers of English is by far the United States, home to approximately two-third of the world's native speakers of English. The country second on the list is the United Kingdom. The large difference in population between the two countries, along with their contrasting economic activities, has made American English more of a major dialect and British English a secondary model of World English.

The typical American English spoken natively is referred to as **General American English (GAE)**. It was commonly defined to be the speech of native English speakers of the upper Middle West United States, neither the types of speech usually observed in the Southeast, New York City, nor in eastern New England. However, recent years have witnessed a shift in its definition. Today, GAE covers multiple of variations without any of the stereotyped features of regional speech.

The primary variety of standard British English speech is termed **Received Pronunciation (RP)**. It shows no regional variation and is typical of the upper-middle class, though it is spoken natively by only about 3 to 5% of the people in the United Kingdom. This speech type was used by the upper class of the southeast midland and was commonly heard at Oxford and Cambridge Universities. RP was regarded as the accent of education, prestige, authority, social status, and economic power. It was once called as "BBC English," though BBC announcers recently have been known to use a wider variety of accents. Today, as a result of change in traditional values, attitudes toward the RP accent are changing.

Some noticeable features distinguish the sound system of GAE from RP. Here is a joke demonstrating a difference in consonant pronunciation between the two sound systems.

055: Snow White Joke

Question: What did the clerk tell Snow White when she complained that her photographs were not ready yet?
Answer: Someday your prints will come.

Behind this joke is a unique GAE feature; the two-consonant cluster /ns/ is likely to be pronounced as a three-consonant cluster /nts/. Therefore, "prince" and "prints" sound almost the same in GAE, which is the key to the joke above. As to vowel sounds, such pairs as *cot/caught* and *don/dawn* are usually pronounced identically, which is not the case in RP.

§2 Segmental or suprasegmental?

It is commonly said that correct pronunciation is one of the keys to establishing effective and successful communication. However, what do we mean by "correct pronunciation"? The term sometimes sounds too general and ambiguous. It definitely refers to some sound system in the language.

The English sound system constitutes two types of features: segmental and suprasegmental. **Segmental features** involve pronunciation of individual sounds, either vowels or consonants. **Suprasegmental features** extend beyond individual sounds, such factors as intonation patterns, rhythm and stress, in longer stretches of discourse.

In communication-oriented English learning, errors on the segmental level may be considered **local errors**, or those that will not cause major misunderstandings among listeners. On the other hand, errors on the suprasegmental level may be regarded as **global errors**, or those that can have a big impact on whether speakers accurately convey their intended messages.

This by no means implies that learners may drop the commitment to learning segmental features. Both aspects must be given equal weight in pronunciation learning and practice, which is the rationale for pronunciation practice. This challenge is sure to promote correct pronunciation in students.

The following are some approaches to teaching the English sound system. Methods of teaching segmental features are discussed first, followed by discussions on teaching the suprasegmental aspects of spoken English.

1 Segmental features

Teaching segmental features involves teaching each individual sound in the vowel and consonant inventories. Here are some examples of how segmental aspects of the English sound system can be taught.

056: Segmental (1/7)
(aspiration of stop voiceless sounds)

Students say the word "pen" with a strip of paper held in front of their mouths. When properly pronounced, a big puff of air forces the paper to move.

This activity serves to raise students' awareness of aspirated stop consonants. Stop consonants, in particular the voiceless stops /p/, /t/, and /k/, are pronounced with a strong airstream at the beginning of words, such as "pen," "time," and "come."

Aspiration does not occur when voiceless stop consonants are located in the middle or at the end of words, such as "s<u>p</u>in" or "shee<u>p</u>." However, a strong aspiration does occur even in the middle of words, such as "a<u>pp</u>eal," "a<u>tt</u>end," and "a<u>k</u>in," in which voiceless stop consonants are followed by stressed vowels.

VARIATION
- Instead of the strip hanging in front of a mouth, a candle can also be used. The aspirated release of stop consonants blows it out.

057: Segmental (2/7)
(minimal-pair practice: voiced or voiceless consonants)

The teacher pronounces the following pairs of words written on the board. Students closely observe the common differences between each pair and repeat after the model.

{ vase /<u>v</u>eis/
{ face /<u>f</u>eis/

{ zeal /<u>z</u>i:l/
{ seal /<u>s</u>i:l/

{ gin /<u>dʒ</u>in/
{ chin /<u>tʃ</u>in/

{ dime /<u>d</u>aim/
{ time /<u>t</u>aim/

{ either /i:<u>ð</u>ər/
{ ether /i:<u>θ</u>ər/

{ allusion /əlu:<u>ʒ</u>ən/
{ Aleutian /əlu:<u>ʃ</u>ən/

{ buy /<u>b</u>ai/
{ pie /<u>p</u>ai/

{ good /<u>g</u>ud/
{ could /<u>k</u>ud/

This practice is so-called **minimal-pair practice**. A **minimal pair** is a set of two words with different meanings that differ in only one segment of pronunciation. Accordingly, the above pairs are all minimal pairs.

Speech sounds fall into the following two groups: voiced or voiceless sounds. Voiced sounds are pronounced with vibration of the vocal cords, and voiceless sounds are produced without this vibration. All vowels are voiced in English.

Some consonants have voiced and voiceless pair partners (i.e., they are the same in where and how the sounds are produced, and differ only in voicing). Each pair of words in the above includes such partners (the top one is voiced; the bottom one is voiceless). They lend themselves well to developing the consciousness of voicing.

Students can see if the sounds are voiced or voiceless by feeling their throats. Another way to distinguish between voiced and voiceless sounds is to place both hands firmly on the ears. When voiced sounds are produced, we will hear a deep boom in our heads or feel its vibration. This will not occur with the voiceless sounds.

058: Segmental (3/7)
(minimal-pair practice: difficult sounds)

Students practice the following four pairs of words shown on the board, so that they will learn to distinguish sounds between each pair (when having problems in those sounds).

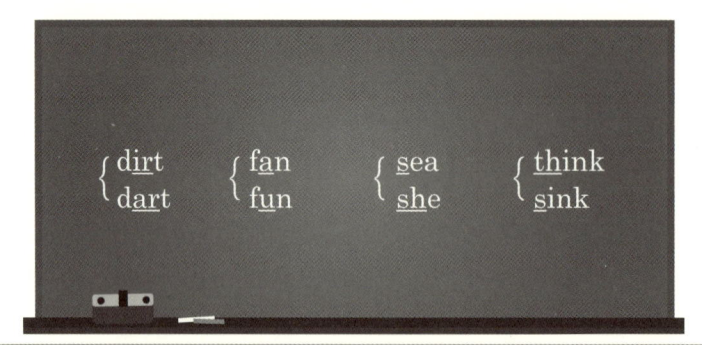

$$\left\{\begin{array}{l}\text{d}\underline{\text{i}}\text{rt}\\ \text{d}\underline{\text{a}}\text{rt}\end{array}\right. \quad \left\{\begin{array}{l}\text{f}\underline{\text{a}}\text{n}\\ \text{f}\underline{\text{u}}\text{n}\end{array}\right. \quad \left\{\begin{array}{l}\underline{\text{s}}\text{ea}\\ \underline{\text{sh}}\text{e}\end{array}\right. \quad \left\{\begin{array}{l}\underline{\text{th}}\text{ink}\\ \underline{\text{s}}\text{ink}\end{array}\right.$$

Minimal-pair practice is useful for helping learners distinguish specific sounds they find hard to recognize as different. The first pair above can be practiced if students have a problem distinguishing between /ə:r/ (top) and /a:r/ (bottom) (/r/ is most likely to be pronounced in GAE), and the other pairs can be used to practice differences between, /æ/ and /ʌ/, /s/ and /ʃ/, /θ/ and /s/, respectively.

English learners with similar L1 background often share the same problems in distinguishing English sounds. For Arabic native speakers, such a challenge would be the difference between /p/ and /b/ at the beginning of words, so they would probably say, "There are some bears in the garden" when meaning to say, "There are some pears in the garden."

For German native speakers, a common problem is distinguishing /dʒ/ and /tʃ/ at the beginning of words, so they would say, "I am choking" instead of, "I am joking." This is exactly the type of situation where minimal-pair practice can be seen.

VARIATION

- For those students who have difficulty distinguishing particular sounds, a **tongue twister** is often used in a language class besides minimal pair practice. For example, the following can be repeated to learn to pronounce /s/ and /ʃ/ sounds distinctively:
  - She sells seashells by the seashore.

059: Segmental (4/7)
(minimal-pair practice: "a cap" or "a cup")

First:
The teacher writes the words "CAP" and "CUP" side by side wide apart on the board.

CAP   CUP

Second:
Student A stands in the front facing the class. The teacher stands in the back and mimes putting on a cap or drinking tea.

Third:
The student says "CAP" or "CUP" according to the mime. Other students, seated facing forward, raise their right or left hands according to which word they think they heard the student say.

This minimal-pair practice is different from the foregoing two examples: Students here need to understand the meanings of the words in the pair. The activity helps students distinguish the correct pronunciation of vowels included in "cap" and "cup." It is self-evident to the student standing in front which word was intended. Before starting, the teacher can show the model pronunciation with students repeating after her several times.

VARIATION

- Instead of acting out, the teacher stands in the back with a card that reads "cap" on one side and "cup" on the other. The student in front says "CAP" or "CUP" according to which side the teacher shows.

060: Segmental (5/7)
(with the help of realia in a meaningful context)

T : (*showing a toy train to students*) Now, class, take a look at here. What is it? A toy...what?
S$_1$: Train.

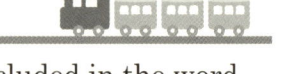

In this example, the two-consonant cluster /tr/ included in the word "train" is targeted. However, the teacher does not have students practice the target sound directly, for example, by saying "Let's see if you make /tr/ sound correctly. Repeat after me..."

With no practice of this, the teacher first has students focus on the conveyance of meaning and it is a good way to check on the pronunciation as it is naturally produced. Words used for this purpose must be familiar to learners in order for the practice to be useful and well accepted. Realia or props can be replaced with pictures or drawings.

061: Segmental (6/7)
(in the context)

T : Let's go over how to say each day of the week. Sunday comes after Saturday. What comes after Thursday?
S$_1$: Friday.
T : Now, let's do some math. Two plus six makes eight. Then, two plus two makes what?
S$_2$: Four.
T : Next, some practice with numbers. Three comes before four. What comes before six?
S$_3$: (*drifting off*)...Yes...Uh...the morning paper.
Class: (*Laughs.*)

The teacher in this example is trying to ensure that students produce /f/ sound correctly. However, she realizes their implicit ability because they concentrate on what to say rather than how to say it. Instead of eliciting words in which the target sound is present straightaway, this activity first calls attention to other words and then to the target words. This consideration makes the activity unique.

🗨 Variation

- Students make a short sentence by using a word with the target sound. When they complete their sentences, they can orally present their work. In this case as well, they focus on getting the messages across to the audience.

062: Segmental (7/7)
(in a gossip game)

First:
Students at the end of each line receive the following direction written on slips, and repeat it to someone in front of them.

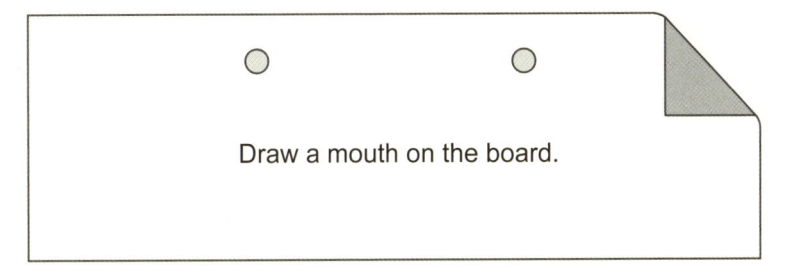

> Draw a mouth on the board.

Second:
Students pass it on orally all the way down to the front. The ones in the front row in each line will do as they are told.

A **gossip game** is useful when the teacher wants to make sure that students can identify a particular sound, and this activity reveals a rather entertaining side of segmental training.

In the example above, the teacher checks whether students can distinguish between the consonants /θ/ and /s/. Some students may draw a "mouse" instead of a "mouth." Similarly, the teacher may use the sentence "Show me your bag" for the difference between /g/ and /k/. Some students may show their *backs* instead.

The interdental sounds /θ/ and /ð/ are distinctive features of the English sound system, so much so that they can be a serious challenge to students. It is always useful to illustrate how they are produced, that is, by protruding the tip of the tongue slightly.

2 Suprasegmental features

Suprasegmental features implies sound characteristics beyond individual sounds, such as stress, rhythm, and intonation patterns. Here are some examples of exercises focusing on those items.

1) Stress

063: Suprasegmental (1/7)
(stressed words: GREEN house or green HOUSE)

T : I have two pictures here. One is a picture of a GREEN house (*stressing GREEN*) and the other one is a green HOUSE (*stressing HOUSE*). (*placing the two picture side by side wide apart on the board*) Now please respond by saying "a GREEN house" or "a green HOUSE." This one is ... (*pointing at the picture of a GREEN house*). Class!
Ss : (*in unison*) A green HOUSE.
T : And that one? (*pointing at the other one*)
Ss : (*in unison*) A GREEN house.
(*after repeating the above exercise a few times*)
T : Now, let's do it individually. This one? Any volunteers?

This activity helps students observe the difference between **compound nouns** (e.g., GREEN house) and nouns modified by an adjective (e.g., green HOUSE) as they pronounced in the context. A GREEN house is where we grow flowers and vegetables, and a green HOUSE is a one painted green.

Here are some other pairs of the same type:

- cold cream
  1) COLD cream (= something we put on the face)
  2) cold CREAM (= something we put on fruit)
- head doctor
  1) HEAD doctor (= psychiatrist)
  2) head DOCTOR (= chief of staff)
- strong man
  1) STRONG man (= man of political influence)
  2) strong MAN (= man with a lot of physical power)

💬 Variation

- Instead of using pictures, the teacher can give words describing or associated with a GREEN house or a green HOUSE, and students say accordingly either of the two. For example, "My friend lives in a..." is for "a green HOUSE" and "Tomatoes are grown in a..." is for the other one.

2) Stress and rhythm

064: Suprasegmental (2/7)
(stress and rhythm: with the help of "chants")

The teacher reads the following sentences one by one as she beats time, such as with clapping hands on the words highlighted in *italics*. Students repeat after her keeping the rhythm.

T:		*Birds*		*eat*		*snails.*
Ss:		*Birds*		*eat*		*snails.*
T:	A	*bird*		*eats*	a	*snail.*
Ss:	A	*bird*		*eats*	a	*snail.*
T:	A	*bird*	will	*eat*	a	*snail.*
Ss:	A	*bird*	will	*eat*	a	*snail.*
T:	A	*bird*	will be	*eating*	a	*snail.*
Ss:	A	*bird*	will be	*eating*	a	*snail.*
T:	A	*bird*	should have	*eaten*	a	*snail.*
Ss:	A	*bird*	should have	*eaten*	a	*snail.*
T:	A	*bird*	should have been	*eating*	a	*snail.*
Ss:	A	*bird*	should have been	*eating*	a	*snail.*

This drill is called "**chants**." In English sentences, **stress** usually falls on **content words** (e.g., nouns, main verbs, adverbs, adjectives, interrogative pronouns), whereas **function words** (e.g., articles, prepositions, auxiliaries, personal pronouns, conjunctions) are usually unstressed. Interestingly enough, stresses occur at fixed intervals. This explains the **rhythm** of English speech. English is a **stress-timed language**, and the length of time needed to say a sentence depends on the number of stressed words it contains.

In each of the five sentences above, stress falls on the three content words: "bird(s)," "eat(s) (eating, eaten)," and "snail(s)." Thus, those sentences are uttered with a 1-2-3 beat. To keep this sentence rhythm, unstressed "a," "will," "will be," "should have," and "should have been," which are all function words, will be pronounced in a quicker, or reduced manner ("should have" and "should have been" may sound like "shoulda" and "shouldabe," respectively). Therefore, "chants" with its accompanying rhythmic beat enables students to learn this significant feature of English speech rather easily.

"Chants" appears to have a beneficial effect on students who natively speak a **syllable-timed language**, such as Japanese, Korean, Spanish, and Polish. In these languages, each syllable receives the same timing and length, and as a result, the number of syllables in a sentence determines the time it takes to pronounce.

3) Prominence

065: Suprasegmental (3/7)
(prominence: stress on emphasized words)

Students think about the situations where the following three responses shown on the board are likely to occur.

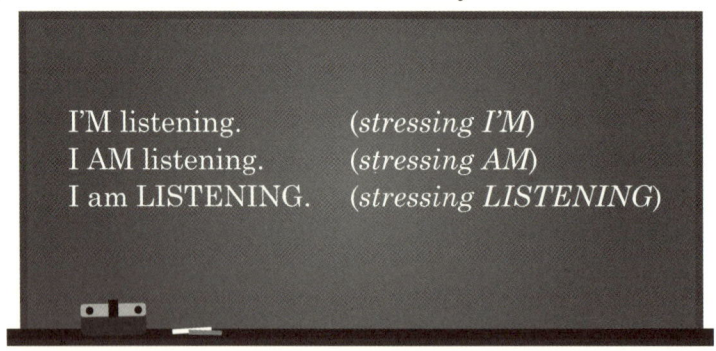

> I'M listening.   (*stressing I'M*)
> I AM listening.   (*stressing AM*)
> I am LISTENING.   (*stressing LISTENING*)

Generally, content words are usually stressed and function words are unstressed. However, at times, the speaker's intentions, or state of mind, take precedence, and stress may occur on words s/he wants to emphasize. The activity here is for students to build their awareness of this phenomenon, or as is often referred to as **prominence**.

The above examples are the most likely responses to the following:

- "Who's listening?"
  "I'M listening. (= I don't know about others.)"
- "Why aren't you listening?" or "Listen to me."
  "I AM listening. (= I am all ears.)"
- "What are you doing?"
  "I am LISTENING. (= I am not singing.)"

After the teacher's model presentation of the three patterns of questions and responses, students may practice them in pairs.

Below is an example in which stress falls on a preposition. The speaker's concern is whether addressees agree or disagree with a tax hike.

- Are you all FOR the tax hike or AGAINST it?

066: Suprasegmental (4/7)
(prominence: stress on new information)

Students work in pairs to think about which words will be stressed in the following context shown on the board. They then perform the lines with their partners.

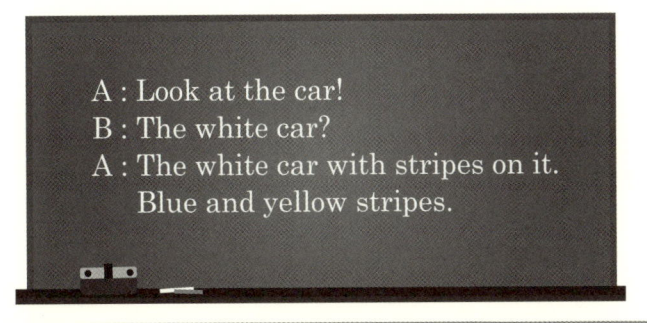

> A : Look at the car!
> B : The white car?
> A : The white car with stripes on it.
>   Blue and yellow stripes.

Here is another example where stress does not necessarily fall on content words. In the example above, stress will be placed on words that are brought up as new pieces of information in the flow of communication.

At the sentence level, the primary stress appears on a content word toward the end of a sentence. This suggests that for "The white car?" in the second line, "car" would receive the primary stress if the speaker's thoughts, or intentions, are not taken into account. In the example above, however, "white" is more stressed because it is a new piece of information. Likewise, in the last line, "blue and yellow" receives more stress than "stripes."

Obviously, in the first line, "car" is more stressed and in the third line, "stripes" is more stressed than other words in their respective lines.

4) Intonation

067: Suprasegmental (5/7)
(intonation patterns in tag questions)

Students in pairs observe the following two dialogs between A and B, and note how intonation goes at the end of tag questions. They then act out the dialogs.

Dialog 1 (*about the holiday weekend*)
  A : You said you'd visit Paris. How was the weather?
  B : Amazing!
  A : You had a nice weekend, didn't you?
  B : Oh, yes.

Dialog 2 (*about the holiday weekend*)
  A : You said you'd visit Paris. How was the weather?
  B : A bit chilly.
  A : You had a nice weekend, didn't you?
  B : Oh, yes.

When people speak, they usually modulate their voices; they raise or lower the pitch, pronounce some syllables more loudly than others, and change their speech rhythm. This phenomenon is termed **intonation**.

Getting to perform a dialog is not just reading aloud. The exercise here helps students become mindful of differences in intonation between the two tag questions.

In **tag questions**, we can express exact meanings by intonation. When we are not seeking any particular information, or when we are sure of the answer, **falling intonation** is applied. When we need some information, or when we are not sure of the answer, rising intonation is used. In Dialog 1, A ends the underlined question with falling intonation because A is certain of B's response from the context. In Dialog 2, A is doubtful whether B really had a nice weekend, and the sentence ends with **rising intonation**.

068: Suprasegmental (6/7)
(intonation patterns: three types)

Students in pairs observe the following three different dialogs. Each pair discusses how differently the three "whats" are pronounced and then performs the dialogs.

Dialog 1
  A: I saw a good movie.
  B: What? (= What movie did you see?)
  A: *Japanese Story*. It's an Australian movie.

Dialog 2
  A: I saw a good movie.
  B: What? (= I didn't hear you. Could you say that again?)
  A: I said, "I saw a good movie."

Dialog 3
  A: I saw a good movie.
  B: What? (= I don't believe you. You are always saying you don't like the movies.)
  A: Oh, believe me.

(Adapted from Celce-Murcia et al. 2000:212)

The three "whats" have different meanings from each other, and are pronounced with contrasting intonations to convey them.

In Dialog 1, B says "What?" with falling intonation, as is usually the case for interrogative sentences starting with wh-words and "how." In Dialog 2, B could not catch what A said and just wants B to repeat it. Therefore, B says "What?" with rising intonation.

Besides the functions mentioned in the last exercise (067), intonation also conveys attitudes or emotions, such as love, hate, satisfaction, disappointment, excitement, boredom, happiness, and sadness. Although regional and individual variation in real-life speech does occur, intonation still involves definite patterns and rules.

In Dialog 3, the reaction of B to what A said is one of amazement and disbelief, and B thus pronounces "What?" emotionally and emphatically with a strong rising intonation.

5) Back-chaining

069: Suprasegmental (7/7)
(back-chaining)

T : First listen to this carefully. (*Pronounces the following sentence and the class listen.*)
"How many times have you been to New York?"
Now class, repeat after me. "to New *York?*"
Ss : "to New *York?*"
T : "have *been* to New *York?*"
Ss : "have *been* to New *York?*"
T : "How many *times* have you *been* to New *York?*"
Ss : "How many *times* have you *been* to New *York?*"

Italicized words are stressed in the sentence.

This activity is intended to ease difficulties in natural production of target sentences. When the teacher has students repeat a sentence, she typically breaks it down into smaller parts. She then starts with the first part of the sentence and adds the following parts one after another. This is a general way to help learners pronounce target sentences.

However, repeating like this can be boring and tiresome. To overcome this problem, and to keep the practice challenging (and fun as well), the teacher uses the "**back-chaining**" technique.

As outlined above, students start with the last part of the sentence and work backwards one bit at a time to the beginning. This step-by-step procedure can prevent them from becoming disengaged by the simple repetition.

In fact, a bigger benefit of back-chaining is its effectiveness in maintaining the correct and natural English intonation throughout the practice. This is because the intonation patterns of an English sentence are determined by the word receiving major sentence stress toward the end of the sentence ("*York*" in the example above).

§3 Sound modifications

Sound modifications may occur in any language people speak. They occur when special sounds are connected to one another in words, phrases, or sentences in a natural flow of spoken languages.

Sound modifications are so common in spoken English that they can play a role in jokes on daily language use. This fact is well-endorsed by the following example.

A student approached the librarian saying, "I would like to borrow 'Of My Cement' by Steinbeck." The student's misunderstanding was perhaps caused by the similar sounds between "Of My Cement" and "Of Mice and Men." The anecdote shows how common and influential sound modifications are in everyday speech.

This section discusses activities to make students conscious of sound modifications in English speech and help improve their listening and speaking skills.

1 Flapping

070: Flapping of the intervocalic /t/

The teacher explains that /t/ sound between vowels is pronounced like /d/ in a casual speech. Students consider which /t/ sound will be pronounced in that manner in the following conversation. There will be seven cases.

> Patty: Tom, what are you doing this evening?
> Tom: Eating alone. What about you, Patty?
> Patty: Well, Mat and I are meeting the Rods for dinner. Can you come?
> Tom: Cool! Thanks for inviting me.

(Adapted from Celce-Murcia et al. 2000:73)

The focus here is on the unique language feature termed "**intervocalic /t/**" (/t/ sandwiched between vowels) or "**flapped /t/**." The flapping occurs particularly when the vowel before the /t/ sound is more stressed than the following vowel, in such words as "beauty" and "city." Consequently, such pairs of words as "latter and ladder" and "putting and pudding" sound almost identical and are inherently difficult to distinguish.

The flapped /t/ is commonly transcribed as /D/ or /ſ/, but other signs are also used in some dictionaries, such as /t̬/ and /ṯ/. This allophonic feature of /t/ was long considered typical of GAE, but the general consensus is that it is noticeable among young native speakers of English in other parts of the world.

The flapped /t/ can be found not only within word, but also between words in a sentence. Here are some examples:

- Get out!   →   /gèDáut/,
- Let it go!   →   /léDətgóu/.

Accordingly, flapping is expected to occur at the following seven spots in the sample dialog above (indicated with underlines).

> Patty : Tom, wha_t_ are you doing this evening?
> Tom : Ea_t_ing alone. Wha_t_ about you, Pa_tt_y?
> Patty : Well, Ma_t_ and I are mee_t_ing the Rods for dinner. Can you come?
> Tom : Cool! Thanks for invi_t_ing me.

2 Linking

071: Linking

Each student asks three different classmates the following question and writes down the responses in the workseet.

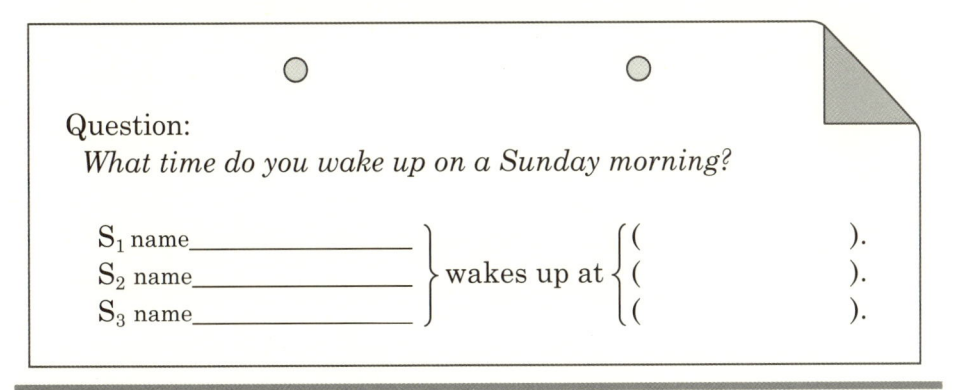

Question:
What time do you wake up on a Sunday morning?

S₁ name_____
S₂ name_____ } wakes up at { ( ).
S₃ name_____   ( ).
                                        ( ).

This activity is oriented for the students to focus on and practice "linking" in a meaningful context. **Linking** is a type of sound modification and is defined as a way of joining, or linking, two words in a natural and smooth flow of spoken English. When linking occurs, these two words do not always sound the same as those pronounced individually.

In the above question—*What time do you wake up on a Sunday morning?*— the target cases of linking include the following:

1) A consonant followed by the identical consonant

When the consonant at the end of a word is identical to the beginning consonant of the following word, the two consonants are uttered as one long consonant. Thus, /t/ in "what" and /t/ in "time" in the question are usually pronounced as one /t/.

2) A consonant followed by a vowel

When a word that ends with a consonant is followed by a vowel in the next word, the consonant sounds like part of the following word. As a result of this, what occurs in the above is as follows:

- "wake up on a" → /wèikʌpənə/ rather than /weik/, /ʌp/, /ɔn/ and /ə/.

3 Assimilation

072: Assimilation

Each student asks three different classmates the following question and writes down the responses in the workseet.

Question:
Where would you like to live, in Cairo, in New York, or in Paris?

S₁ name_____
S₂ name_____ } would like to live in { ( ).
S₃ name_____   { ( ).
                                                 { ( ).

This activity is oriented for the students to learn and practice what is described as assimilation. **Assimilation** is a case where a sound changes and becomes more like another sound that follows (or precedes) it.

In the question—*Where would you like to live, in Cairo, in New York, or in Paris?*— the target assimilation items include the following:

1) Palatalization

When a word that ends with consonants /t/ or /d/ is followed by the consonant /j/, they become /tʃ/ or /dʒ/, respectively. Assimilation of this type is termed **palatalization**. This is so called because in this case the alveolar consonants /t/ and /d/ are made further back in the mouth cavity near to the hard palate (/t/ and /d/ are usually made at the tooth ridge), where the semi-vowel /j/ is produced. Therefore, what occurs here is as follows:

- "would you" → /wudʒə/, not /wud/ and /jə/.

2) Assimilation of nasals

The alveolar nasal /n/ is changed into the other nasals /m/ or /ŋ/ in a casual speech according to the sound that immediately follows. This is particularly true for the /n/ at the end of function words. That is, when an "in" is followed by a bilabial consonant, such as /m/, /p/, and /b/, the "in" is pronounced /ɪm/, and when an "in" is followed by a velar consonant, such as /k/ and /g/, the "in" becomes /ɪŋ/. Thus, what occurs in the example above is as follows:

- "in Cairo"   → /ɪŋ káɪrou/,
- "in New York"   → /ɪn njùː jɔ́ːk/ (no assimilation occurring here),
- "in Paris"   → /ɪm pǽrəs/.

4 Jokes to illustarate sound modifications

073: Knock-knock jokes

Students read out the following joke on the board and think about why it is funny.

> A: Knock, knock.
> B: Who's there?
> A: Juno.
> B: Juno who?
> A: Juno what time it is?

This is an example of a **knock-knock joke**. It provides the teacher with a good opportunity to explain unique features of sound modifications in a humorous setting. The punch line (or the last line that makes us laugh) is funny because two words or more produce unexpected sound similarities based on pronunciation modification.

The point in the joke above is the similarity in sound between "Juno" and "Do you know" because of the effect of palatalization (see page 98).

The standard format of knock-knock jokes has five lines as shown above. This type of joke is said to have been popular among children and adults in the United Kingdom and United States since the 1930s, and its prototype is found in Shakespeare's Macbeth, in Act II, scene iii.

Here are some further examples:

    A: Knock, knock.
    B: Who's there?
    A: Jamaica.
    B: Jamaica who?
    A: <u>Jamaica</u> Mistake.   (≒ Did you make a)

    A: Knock, knock.
    B: Who's there?
    A: Eugenes.
    B: Eugenes who.
    A: <u>Eugenes</u> need washing..   (≒ Your jeans)

    A: Knock, knock.
    B: Who's there?
    A: Felix.
    B: Felix who.
    A: <u>Felix</u> my lollipop again, I'll thump him.   (≒ If he licks)

EXTENSION

- Students in pairs can search the Internet for knock-knock jokes (there are hundreds of them), present some orally to the class taking the roles of A and B as shown above. Each pair then explains the punch lines, or gives the class a chance to put on their thinking caps.

CHAPTER SIX

On Integration

Thus far, discussions have focused on how to handle the four major skill areas (listening, speaking, reading, and writing) individually. However, this does not suggest that one area can or should be taught in isolation, as may be implied in the preceding chapters. In authentic language use, opportunities requiring just one skill are rare. Rather, multiple skills are put to practical use simultaneously and consecutively in daily communication. When a message is received on the phone, for instance, it is jotted down, and later the content is orally conveyed to the person it concerns.

The final goal of teaching a second or foreign language is to enable learners to completely activate their language skills in situations in which they have to function independently. Consequently, the teacher needs to ensure whenever possible that multiple skills are continuously developed, and hence expose learners to a large amount of authentic language. The premise is that, for language items (e.g., grammar, vocabulary, and sentences) to be reinforced in our minds, we have to not just hear, but speak; not only hear and speak but also read and write. Each skill strengthens the others, so students will become more competent language users.

This chapter examines some model sequences of activities that engage students in multiple-skill language use within a classroom setting. Some can be easily built in the daily class schedules and routines using a course book. Others are content- and task-based, and owing to their nature, may take longer and therefore call for thoughtful advance course planning before execution.

Whether the assignments are all-purpose course-book based or content- and task-based, they will add interest to daily classwork and present students fresh challenges.

§1 Using a course book

In this section, multiple-skill activities using a course book are introduced and methods for their successful conduct are explained in detail.

1 Repeating a group of sentences in different words

> **074: Repeating a group of sentences in different words**
>
> Students work in pairs.
> First:
> One student in each pair reads silently a short meaningful segment of sentences from the course book.
>
> Second:
> The student paraphrases the segment to the other without referring to the text.
>
> Third:
> Students exchange each other's role and work on a new segment.

This activity is an application of "**read and look up**" technique, with which students first read a sentence silently and repeat it orally without seeing the text.

One student here interprets the meaning of the segment, and reads it aloud trying to convey the content concisely. The focus is integration of word recognition with comprehension and speaking and pronunciation skills. The student needs to use inflection and tone of voice, and reads in thought units to help the other student grasp the ideas aurally.

For this multiple-skill exercise, any genre of reading materials can be used, including persuasive, argumentative, or narrative texts. This activity is appropriate when students read the text for the first time. Therefore, the task can be included in pre-reading activities (see page 53).

2 Asking questions in pairs

> **075: Asking questions in pairs**
>
> First:
> Students read the text. They then formulate and write down three wh-questions about the content and their answers.
>
> Second:
> They split into pairs and one student gives the questions to the other, who tries to find the answers in the text.

> Third:
> Students change the roles of each pair.

Any genre of text can also be used for this task. The exercise is appropriate for reviewing previously learned materials, and can be easily incorporated in daily classroom settings.

In the first step, students engage in **intensive reading*** (refer to the footnote) of the text while framing and jotting down questions and model answers.

In the second and third steps, one student in each pair speaks and the other listens. This time, the listener is involved in **extensive reading*** while spotting key words, phrases, or sentences needed to answer the questions. Thus in the activity above, students perform two types of reading.

3 A post-reading activity

> **076: As a post-reading activity**
>
> First:
> Students freely imagine the future development of a story after its end in the text and write down their ideas in a few short sentences. The funnier and crazier the ideas are, the better.
>
> Second :
> The teacher asks one student (S_1) to read his/her writing out loud.
>
> Third:
> The teacher asks another student to summarize what S_1 said.
>
> Fourth:
> S_1 writes what s/he said on the board, and the other students read it for confirmation.

This is a perfect example of how an open-ended post-reading activity (see page 55) can easily be transformed into a multi-skill language task. The text that works best here is a narrative with a definite story line.

---

*Intensive reading: reading in most cases at a slower rate, intended to gain a higher degree of understanding than extensive reading.
*Extensive reading: reading in quantity to gain a general understanding of the text, intended to develop regular reading habit.

In this activity, students engage in reading, writing, listening, and speaking. The writing involved here has no restrictions; consequently, by the fourth step, all the class will be very curious to know the stories their peers have invented, and will attentively read what is written on the board.

Please note that first S_1 gives an oral presentation of his/her writing (in the second step above) and next writes it on the board. This sequence must be closely observed. Thus, the other students focus on listening, and then on reading to confirm what they think they heard. It would defeat the purpose if the presentation was given in the wrong order.

Inviting predictions about what occurs next can also be included in pre- and during-reading activities. As a pre-reading activity, students can predict the content of the text from the title or illustrations. As a during-reading activity, they can guess what occurs next in the story line, for example, in the succeeding paragraphs, page or section.

Before starting the third step, each student can first rehearse in pairs or in small groups. This is appropriate for those too shy to speak in front of the class.

4 Impersonation of a main character

077: Impersonation of a main character

First:
Students read the following materials in the worksheet.

In spring 2008, the polar bear was placed on the endangered species list. Endangered species are animals facing extinction from their natural habitat in the foreseeable future. The polar bear is the first animal that has been classified as endangered primarily due to global warming.

Global warming is caused by carbon dioxide and other greenhouse gases trapped in the atmosphere. Heating homes, driving cars, and burning garbage all require fossil fuels that lead to global warming. The polar bear's habitat is more vulnerable to global warming than many other species. Polar bears live mainly on sea ice in the Arctic. This is where they hunt for fish and build up fat reserves.

The World Wildlife Fund estimates that 25% of the

> *arctic sea ice has disappeared in the past 30 years. It is not just the polar bear that is at risk in the Arctic, but every species of plant, animal, and insect in that region is threatened by global warming.*

Second:
Students form groups of four.

Third:
Two students in each group play the roles of "polar bears" (mother and cub), and the remaining two play "reporters" (one is an interviewer and the other is a "recorder").

Fourth:
The "reporters" interview the "bears" about their life in the Arctic in order to write an article.

(Adapted from Endangered species reading: Polar bear makes the list)

In this example, students play the roles of characters from the reading materials and interact with each other. The "bears" have the opportunity to talk about topics not referred to in the materials and have leeway to respond creatively to keep the interview going. Students could find this group work interesting and engaging.

Depending on the materials, interviewees could be anything: a flower, tree, or an insect, needless to say, an A-list celebrity (even a dead one) in areas of such as sports, music, or film industry. For the use in activities of this type, descriptive passages from stories of flora and fauna, historical stories, anecdotes, travelogues, and diaries are certainly recommended. Abstract stories may not be workable.

VARIATION
- Students can work in pairs with one participant being a "reporter" and the other being the interviewee.

§2 Beyond a course book

In this section, multiple-skill activities beyond using a course book are introduced and methods for their successful implementation are explained in detail.

1 Using a comic strip

> **078: Using a comic strip**
>
> A comic strip with four panels is used. Students get into groups of four, each group consisting of members S_1, S_2, S_3, and S_4.
>
> First:
> The teacher cuts a comic strip into four individual panels.
>
> Second:
> He shows one of them to S_1 from each group. Then S_1s return to their groups and talk about the panel. The other students in each group listen and take notes. (The same procedure is called again; S_2s see the next panel and they talk about it in their groups, and S_3s and S_4s follow suit.)
>
> Third:
> S_1, S_2, S_3, and S_4 in the same group meet, and work out the story line of the original comic strip. (In each group, one will be the recorder who writes it down, and another will be the spokesperson in the next step.)
>
> Fourth:
> The spokespersons for each group take turns orally presenting their stories to the class.
>
> Fifth:
> The recorders for each group write them on the board.

The order in which each panel is presented needs to be different from the original. All students in each group have opportunities to actively listen, speak, or give descriptions, as well as to take and read notes. Throughout this process, attention is called to the messages being conveyed.

In the fourth step, students listen intently while trying to determine the story line other groups have devised. Because this is a creative and open-ended writing, they know that a variety of stories will be presented. In the last step, they read the board very closely, trying to ascertain if what they thought they heard was correct. Of course, what counts is actual language use involved in the process. The final outcomes they produce are of peripheral interest to the teacher.

VARIATION

- Instead of using panels from a comic strip, the teacher can tell four parts of a story in random order to S_1, S_2, S_3, and S_4.

2 Applying for an EFL program

079: Applying for an EFL program

First:
Students divide into groups of three. In each group, S_1 takes the role of a representative of an overseas EFL program and interviews S_2 and S_3, who are both students applying for the last space in the program.

Second:
S_2 and S_3 write their reasons for applying in 50 words to convince S_1 (the representative).

Third:
S_1 reads the reasons written by S_2 and S_3, and consider questions to ask in their interview.

Fourth:
S_1 interviews S_2 and S_3 one after another.

Recently, there has been a substantial increase in the number of those attending overseas language-learning programs. Thus, this group assignment may be relevant and beneficial to students.

The "interviewees" may write something to appeal to the interviewer, such as what features of the program address the individual needs. This activity can be used as a further extension of the authentic resume-writing activity on pages 75 to 76.

3 Newspaper reporting

080: Newspaper reporting

First:
Students search through a newspaper for an interesting and informative article to introduce to other students.

Second:
They write a summary of the piece.

Third:
Each student orally presents his/her summary to the class with accompanying pictures if available.

Fourth:
A question-and-answer session is conducted between the speaker and audience.

In the first step, students read extensively, while searching the paper for appropriate news story.

In the second step, once they have chosen their news items, they shift their attention to the details. Reading between the lines may be necessary. They then prepare summaries, which become the scripts for the oral presentations in the next step. In this process, students may have to paraphrase the original vocabulary or structures to make it more comprehensible. This requires in-depth reading.

In the third step, students concentrate on speech production, perhaps with the aid of visual materials, so that the audiences can understand them easily.

What occurs in the fourth step is an interaction of a more authentic type among students because it is open-ended and unpredictable. Thus, they need to respond to each question on a case-by-case basis.

4 Postcard writing

081: Postcard writing

First:
Students read the following postcard message written on the board or photocopied.

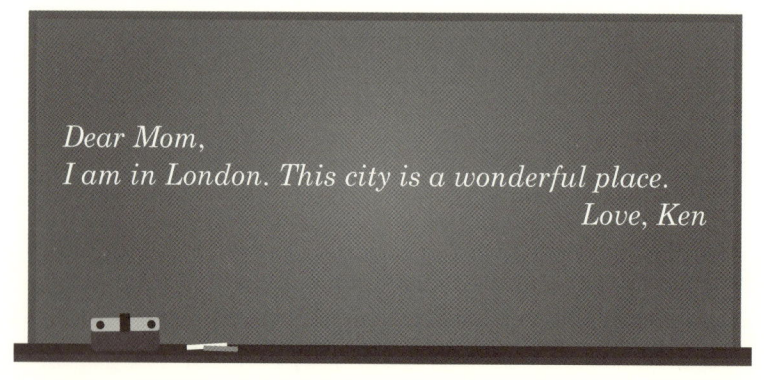

Dear Mom,
I am in London. This city is a wonderful place.
                                              Love, Ken

Second:
The class brainstorms as many questions as possible that Ken's mother will have when she receives this card.

Third:
Students work in groups of four to produce a new version of the postcard message to ease her mind. They must do this in 20 minutes. (One student will be the recorder who writes down the new message, one will be the moderator who makes sure every member takes a turn speaking, one will be the timekeeper, and the last student will be the group spokesperson in the next step.)

Fourth:
After each group creates its version of the message, the spokespersons from each group orally present their versions to the class.

Fifth:
The recorders from each group write their versions on the board.

This activity can be used alone or as an extension of reading materials in a course book, such as travelogues or letters from abroad with descriptions of scenic or historical places.

In the second step, the teacher reminds the class that Ken's mother wants to know everything her son is doing and seeing, as is always the case with mothers, and that the message in the card is too short and uninformative for her (and may even makes her nervous.)

Some of the questions Ken's mother would probably have in mind are as follows:

- Who was Ken with?
- When did Ken write the card?
- Where did Ken go and how?
- What was the weather like?
- Where in London did Ken stay?

In the third step, each student is assigned a job in his/her group. This ensures that every member gets involved in the activity.

VARIATIONS

- Brainstorming may occur in each group instead of in the entire class; the smaller the group, the greater is the likelihood of close relationships and full participation.
- The exercise can be conducted without the sample postcard message. Students

discuss in groups what they would say in letters if they were away on vacation. They then produce messages.
- Students can decide on the place they are "staying at," somewhere they want to visit someday.

5 Conducting a survey

082: Conducting a survey

Students working in pairs jointly perform these tasks.

First:
Decide on a survey topic.

Second:
Prepare a draft of the questionnaire.

Third:
Proofread the draft and rewrite it.

Fourth:
Administer the questionnaire.

Fifth:
Summarize the data.

Sixth:
Make an oral presentation of the findings to the class.

In a **survey**, students employ multiple language skills in a real-life setting in the classroom.

The teacher can show in advance a questionnaire format for the survey to the class, as shown below. In the first step, he gives them a choice of topics to choose from. Students need to be guided so that the topics will be relevant to their educational content and be directly related to their daily lives.

In the second step, students brainstorm ideas on what to ask and create a rough draft.

In the third step, they need to carefully read the draft, examining logical order of questionnaire items (if necessary), sentence structures, grammar, and vocabulary. Here the teacher's guidance may also be needed for the same educational reasons as in the first step.

In the fourth step, students conduct the survey by administering the questionnaire to the respondents directly or by having them complete it independently. Alternatively, students can simply poll the class by asking to raise their hands for the choice that best fits them personally in survey questions.

In the fifth step, each pair collaborates on a written report for the following oral presentation, including how the presentation will be given effectively, for example, by using graphs, charts, and realia.

The topics for this questionnaire activity will derive from those of general interest, such as food, leisure activities (TV watching, internet use, playing sports), and school subjects.

(sample format of a questionnaire)

Snack questionnaire

During the day, when do you feel like a light snack? Tick the box that best suits you.
- ☐ In the morning.
- ☐ In the afternoon.
- ☐ At midnight.
- ☐ At other times (specify   ).

What would you like for a snack then?
- ☐ Cookies/ chocolate/ potato chips.
- ☐ Fruit.
- ☐ Vegetables.
- ☐ Others (specify   ).

Who mostly buys snacks at your house?
- ☐ Parent(s).
- ☐ Yourself.
- ☐ Others (specify   ).

---

6 Group research project

083: Group research project

First:
Each group decides on a theme for its research.

Second:
Assignments are given to each group member, such as collecting data, assembling it, or making an oral presentation.

Third:

Spokespersons from each group make their presentations.

A **research project** provides various linguistic and academic benefits to students as they learn to design and perform the task involved. They should form groups according to their common interests. This should be demanded much for successful accomplishment of the tasks.

In the first step, the teacher can offer a choice of themes for students to choose from for educational reasons. Alternatively, if the project is given toward the end of term, semester, or school year, students can choose a theme from the issues they have studied and taken an interest in from other subjects (e.g., science, history and geography).

The second step is to ensure that all members contribute cooperatively to the project.

Research projects inevitably involve a series of tasks over a fixed time period in which careful and elaborate planning is required. The procedure can be divided chronologically into distinct phases (deciding on the theme, collecting data, assembling the data, writing the first draft, and revising for the last version for the presentation). Therefore, it is highly recommended that the teacher set clear deadlines for completion of each phase of the project ahead of time. This helps students manage their time more effectively.

The benefit from a research project is two-fold: enhancement of content and language knowledge, and development of camaraderie among classmates. The whole process requires both so much time and work so that students will be bursting with pride and finally filled with sense of successful accomplishment.

7 Debate

A **debate** is a discussion about a particular subject or topic. It often continues for a certain period with participants putting forth their arguments for and against the given subject.

084: Debate

First:
The teacher assigns a topic for debate.

Second:
The class is divided into either the pro or con side

Third:
Each side studies the arguments for and against it. While studying arguments, students in each group share ideas to

clarify their strongest and weakest positions. Students then outline what they found.

Forth:
Based on the information collected, students consider how to respond to possible counter-arguments in each group.

Fifth:
The teacher informs of the time limit for presenting the arguments and responding to the counter-arguments on the other side.

The first thing to do as a part of language activity is select a good topic. The teacher may have students brainstorm topics, though they should not have absolute free reign over choosing the topic. They must be guided, so that topics will be relevant to their educational needs.

The pros and cons being weighed by the students, the topic needs to have supporting positions on both sides. In the third step, students read materials carefully, and put together the information collected in written form. In the succeeding steps, students engage in speaking and listening. Thus, multiple-skill language use is ensured.

In case students are not familiar with debate, the teacher can show a sample debate format and useful expressions, such as shown below.

(a debate format)

> Speaker A (pro side):
>   Five minutes to present arguments for the topic
>   (two-minute interval)
> Speaker B (con side):
>   One minute of questions or counter-arguments
> Speaker C (con side):
>   Five minutes to present arguments against the topic
>   (two-minute interval)
> Speaker D (pro side):
>   One minute of questions or counter-arguments
>   (two-minute interval)
> Speaker E (pro side):
>   Five minutes to respond and summarize
> Speaker F (con side):
>   Five minutes to respond and summarize

Here are some debate vocabulary.

>   To state an opinion:
>   *In my opinion...*

>   *I think (feel, believe) that…*
>   *It seems to me that…*
>   *In addition (Furthermore)…*

To have someone repeat or explain:
>   *I don't understand what you mean.*
>   *Could you explain that, please?*
>   *Would you give me an example?*

To agree with someone:
>   *I agree with you.*
>   *That's a good point.*
>   *I see what you mean.*

To disagree with someone:
>   *I disagree.*
>   *That's not the point.*

To persuade someone:
>   *You have to admit that…*
>   *Do you really think that..?*

CHAPTER SEVEN

Vocabulary Games

Games are an important part of a teacher's repertoire, though some teachers are wary of devoting precious classroom time to them. In fact, it should be recognized that games have obvious merits in class, as will be seen below. After all, students, young and old, enjoy playing games. This chapter includes activities that are recreational in nature for students. They can be played at the end of a class period as a filler or as part of a meeting outside regular class.

Students seem to like games for three major reasons. First, they avail themselves of opportunities to get away from "the here and now" of a rigid learning situation. This is particularly true for easily intimidated and self-conscious students. They may tend to worry about their performance in class, but will engage in games in a more expansive mood. For both teachers and students, games can change routines of daily instruction and recharge the batteries when class starts to get monotonous and uninspiring.

Second, games are often team events in which groups of students compete in a healthy atmosphere. Competition is one of our natural inclinations, and language activities can exploit this. Where there is competition, there is always enthusiasm and energy. Points can be awarded to the winning team after each round of games, and at the end of a game session, the teacher can have the class give a round of applause to the group with the most points.

Third, since luck often, if not always, determines who or which team scores well, both strong and weak participants will equally enjoy taking part in a cooperative learning environment. With the entire class laughing and sharing fun moments together, a better rapport is created not only among students but also between them and their teacher.

Therefore, for the last reason (and sometimes if for no other reason than this) in particular, effective games often center on vocabulary items. If they instead focused on one of the four major skills of language, games would not entertain weaker students as much as stronger ones with the fun nature being jeopardized.

For games to be played without any confusion, at the outset the teacher may have to demonstrate how they are meant to work with a few students at the front of the class, so that everyone can see the procedure. Alternatively, she might have participants play one practice round first. This is especially true for competitive games.

There is no need for teachers to run each game as they are described below. They can tailor the formats to suit the needs of their classroom contexts.

1 Pictograph

085: Pictograph

Students see the following pictures shown on the board or the screen and think about what they mean.

A pictograph, or a pictorial symbol for a word or phrase, is the earliest known form of writing, and we can use pictographs to good advantage in a language classroom.

Here each picture corresponds to a certain letter of the alphabet. The leftmost picture "cherries" represents the letter "C" and the next image, "house," represents "H," and so forth. The combined pictures represent the word "CHOCOLATE."

VARIATION
- The pictures can be arranged so that they will stand for short instructions for students to follow. Thus, the teacher will know easily who has solved the pictograph.

EXTENSION
- This game can be used for a treasure hunt. Groups of students have to decipher the first pictograph, and the solution leads them to where the second one is hidden and so on, until the final code reveals the location of a prize.

2 Odd one out

086: Odd one out

Students guess which one of the four words in each group does not belong to the others and why it does not.

DOG MOUSE PELICAN TIGER	DISH FORK KNIFE SPOON	BULL CRAB FISHES ZEBRA

The solutions to the above (from the left to right) are as follows:

- "PELICAN" (The others are mammals.)
- "DISH" (The others are pieces of silverware.)
- "ZEBRA" (The others are signs of the zodiac.)

The phrase "odd one out" means something, or someone, in a group that is different from the others. This is its game version widely played in language classes.

Sometimes there may be more than one solutions to a question if reasonable explanations can be found for them.

By some accounts, the name of the game was that of a weekly quiz program broadcast in the United Kingdom in the early 1980s. In the program, some points were awarded to those who guessed the correct "odd one out" and extra points were given when they stated a satisfactory reason for that. This format can be applicable when students compete among themselves either individually or in groups.

Words belonging together may come from lexical sets such as the following:

- names of capital cities of nations: LONDON, ROME, PARIS, WELLINGTON;
- words starting with stop sounds: BUS, CAT, DOG, TOWN;
- words with double letters in them: BAZ**AA**R, BU**BB**LE, A**CC**IDENT, A**DD**;
- words consisting of symmetric letters: HAM, HOT, MOUTH, WAX.

VARIATION

- The teacher may show students some four-word groups with their respective odd ones out, and has them think about why they stand alone in each group.

3 Hidden commonalities

087: Hidden commonalities

Each box below contains two groups of vocabulary words: Group A and Group B. Students think about what the common feature is among the words in Group A that cannot be found among those in Group B in each box.

Group A	Group B
CAT	DOG
INK	PEN
POND	LAKE
FORTH	BACK

Group A	Group B
BASEBALLS	BASKETBALLS
DOUGHNUTS	TIRES
HEADS	BALLOONS
MELONS	BELL PEPPERS

Group A	Group B
CHICKS	KIWIS
DUCKS	PIGEONS
PIGS	ELEPHANTS
COWS	BULLS

This game is a further extension to "odd one out" because the solution to each game is finding the common factor among the given set of words.

Here the common factors in Group A in each group above (from the top down) are as follows:

- containing hidden prepositions ("at" is in "CAT," "in" in "INK," "on" in "POND," and "for" in "FORTH");
- having something within them (or they are stuffed);
- including birds or animals that "Old MacDonald" kept on his farm.

To make sure that students concentrate on the game, pair words in each box should be gradually revealed, not all at one time.

4 Animal grid

088: Animal grid

Students search the following grid for names of twenty

animals. They are arranged horizontally, vertically, diagonally, or even backward.

Animal Grid

S	G	D	L	M	S	Y	T	O	R	R	P
K	O	I	E	H	O	N	J	T	O	E	P
U	O	R	E	E	A	I	A	T	T	G	K
N	S	E	E	H	R	R	Y	E	A	I	P
Q	P	T	P	C	B	A	D	R	G	T	G
V	X	E	U	E	O	R	A	T	I	W	O
Y	L	P	Z	R	I	N	E	P	L	W	A
E	R	K	N	U	K	S	I	K	L	T	T
P	J	G	B	F	N	E	Z	H	A	K	A
R	O	O	S	T	E	R	Y	T	R	N	C
D	V	V	V	R	V	Q	B	E	A	R	S
I	Z	Y	F	L	O	W	N	B	S	B	Z

Solutions:
"alligator," "bat," "cat," "bear," "deer," "dog," "elephant," "goat," "lion," "otter," "rat," "rhinoceros," "rooster," "sheep," "skunk," "snake," "tiger," "turkey," "wolf," "zebra."

A time limit should be placed on this game. The winner is the student, or group, who finds the largest number of names within that time or the first one to find all twenty animals.

Instead of animal names, other vocabulary sets may be used in the grid, such as household or classroom items, flowers and plants, family and relatives, months and weekdays, famous cities, parts of the body, fruits and vegetables, or basic adjectives.

There are completely web-based sites on the Internet (there is no need to download and install any software) where teachers can create puzzles without spending much time. Puzzlemaker (http://www.discoveryeducation.com) is a popular site with teachers.

Variation

- A feature from crossword puzzles can be incorporated into this game. Students will find the answers to clues given to them, and search for those answers on the grid. For example,

  This is an animal that barks. (Clue for "dog")
  The largest living land animal. (Clue for "elephant")

5 Spelling bee

> **089: Spelling bee**
>
> First:
> The class break into two teams and line up facing each other across the classroom with the teacher standing in front of the two lines.
>
> Second:
> The teacher gives a word for the first student in one line to spell. If the spelling is correct, he gives another word for the first student in the other line to spell.
>
> Third:
> The teacher asks the second student in each line to spell a word and so on back and forth between the groups.
>
> If a word is spelled incorrectly, the student will be out of the game and takes a seat. The same word will then be given to the next student in the other line and back and forth until the right spelling is given.

The spelling bee is one of the earliest known word games. Words for this game can be given orally, or with pictures or drawings.

Participants' spelling ability rather than luck determines the outcome of this game, and some may find it highly stressful. The choice of words, therefore, needs to be carefully considered so that even weak students can enjoy participating.

The procedure for the spelling bee can be followed in other word games.

6 Charades

> **090: Charades**
>
> First:
> The class split in two teams of equal size. For the first round, the first students from each team come to the front.
>
> Second:
> The teacher, standing in the back, shows the two students (standing in the front) an actionable word (verb or noun) in

writing or with a picture, and they take turns enacting it. The remaining students (facing forward) work in teams to identify the word within a limited time.

Third:
The leaders of each team write that word on a slip and give it to the teacher. The team that guesses the word correctly gets a point for the first round.

The second round follows for the second students from each team to act out.

Charades is a game of pantomimes; participants have to let others guess what a word is without speaking, only by action.

This game can apply to all levels of learners, and short phrases, such as titles of books, movies, television programs, or songs, can be used as well as words. To act out these titles, clues may be given by making actions of such as the following:

- twisting the left wrist repeatedly over the open palm of the right hand as if turning pages (to indicate titles of books);
- connecting quickly the thumb and forefinger as if they were a clapperboard (to indicate titles of movies);
- making the letters of first "T" with two hands and then "V" with two fingers (to indicate titles of TV programs);
- pretending to sing (to indicate titles of songs).

7 Scrambled words

091: Scrambled words

Each box below has a list of vocabulary words in the same category, but the letters in each word are scrambled. Students correctly rearrange them.

ATBEELSEVG	DEHA	NOSANIT
oamtot	yee	paresingo
ototap	sone	lizrba
arcort	cekeh	anhga
eclery	worbs	aidin
rnoc	are	hainc

To maintain students' interest, each "word" may be revealed individually so that every student will start afresh each time.

Items in the left group are all "vegetables" as the title "VEGETABLE (also scrambled)" shows: (from the top) tomato, potato, carrot, celery, and corn.

Items in the middle group are parts of the "HEAD": eye, nose, cheek, brows, and ear.

Similarly, the last group consists of names of "NATIONS" in the world: Singapore, Brazil, Ghana, India, and China.

In the example above, the scrambled words in each group belong to a common category, but this is not necessary. After a unit or lesson is over, this vocabulary activity can be performed to review the correct spelling of target vocabulary items.

To help students, some letters can be shown in their correct positions, for example, "**w**eamltroe**n**" for the scrambled "watermelon."

The procedure for the spelling bee can be applied to this game.

8 Missing vowels

092: Missing vowels

Each box below has a list of vocabulary words. The letters in each word are in the correct order but vowels are missing. Students think of the missing vowels and identify the word.

pnppl	rsr	mthmtcs
wtrmln	scssrs	scnc
kwfrt	pncl	hstry
grpfrt	rlr	msc
vcd	stplr	rt

The left group includes names of fruits: (from the top) pineapple, watermelon, kiwifruit, grapefruit, and avocado.

The middle group consists of stationery supplies: eraser, scissors, pencil, ruler, and stapler.

The last group included subjects taught at school: mathematics, science, history, music, and art.

While conducting this activity, each "word (without vowels)" should be shown one at a time so students' attention and interest will be renewed whenever a new word is given. This activity can also be conducted with the same format as the spelling bee.

9 Secret code

093: Secret code

Students decipher the secret message below and follow the instructions it provides.

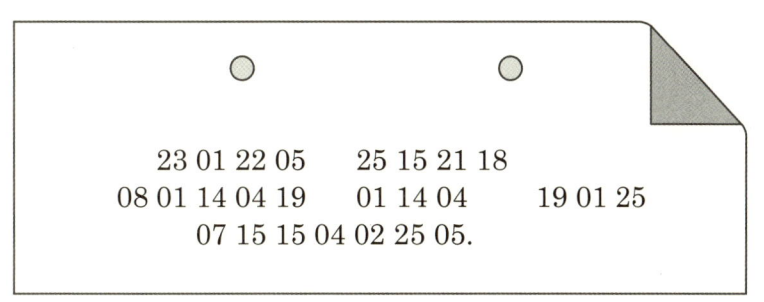

```
    23 01 22 05    25 15 21 18
 08 01 14 04 19    01 14 04       19 01 25
       07 15 15 04 02 25 05.
```

Solution: "Wave your hands and say goodbye."

The key to the example code is of the simplest type; "01" is for A, "02" is for B, and "26" is for Z, but other codes can be used, such as the following:

- "26" is for A, "25" is for B, and "01" is for Z;
- "a" is for B, "b" is for C, and "z" is for A;
- "3/2" (representing "3 minus 2", making 1) is for A, "3/1" ("3 minus 1", making 2) is for B, and "29/3" is for Z.

This game can be organized as a competition among groups in which the first group to perform the instructions hidden in the code wins. It would be great fun having students create their own hidden messages for the class to decode.

EXTENSION
- This game can be incorporated into a treasure hunt. Each group of students has to crack the first code and the solution leads them to the location of the second one, and thus codes are given one after another until a "treasure" is revealed.

10 Key words

094: Key words

First:
Students break into two teams. For the first round, the first students (S_{1s}) from Teams A and B come to the front and stand facing the class.

Second:
The second students (S$_2$s) from each team go to the back of the classroom and stand facing the front.

Third:
The teacher, standing in the back, shows S$_1$s from each team the same secret word written on the back blackboard.

Fourth:
The S$_1$s take turns giving one-word clues to their corresponding S$_2$s, who try to guess the word from the clues.

In the example below, Team A wins in the first round. This is how it proceeds:
  (*The secret word of "glasses" is shown to S$_1$s from each team.*)
    S$_1$ of Team A: (*seeing the word*) Face.
    S$_2$ of Team A: Nose.
    S$_1$ of Team B: (*seeing the word*) Wear.
    S$_2$ of Team B: Makeup.
    S$_1$ of Team A: Pair.
    S$_2$ of Team A: Glasses. (*Wins the round*).

For the second round, S$_1$s return to their teams, and S$_2$s come to the front. The teacher gives S$_2$s another secret word, and the third students from each team guess the word. This time, Team B will be the first to give a clue.

The teacher may show the secret word by holding up a picture of glasses or simply her pair of glasses. Her role may be performed by a student assistant who remains neutral in the game.

Students giving clues stand in the back and those guessing stand in the front, so that the whole class can clearly hear the clues and be involved in the game. This is especially important when the class is rather large.

A limit may be put on the number of opportunities for each team to guess the word. If neither team guesses it correctly within this time, another word is given.

11 Words within a word

095: Words within a word

Students make as many words as possible from letters in a

word given by the teacher.

There are three rules:
- First, students should not use letters more often than they appear in the word.
- Second, students may arrange letters in any order.
- Third, each word must be at least two letters long.

For instance, if the word given is "English," words, such as "hen," "leg," and "shine" are possible.

This game has a time limit. The length of the time limit depends on students' levels of proficiency; perhaps no more than three minutes should be allotted for intermediate students, or they will become restless. A word for this game should contain various letters, especially vowels ("a," "e," "i," "o," and "u").

Points can be awarded according to the number of letters used to make words, for example, two points for two-letter words, three points for three-letter words. This allows participants to compete against each other, either individually or in teams.

Variation
- A phrase instead of a word may be given, for example, "English word." This allows more words to be found. In finding words in a phrase like this, a longer length requirement for words (four letters or more) can be imposed.

12 Matching symbols with meanings

096: Matching symbols with meanings

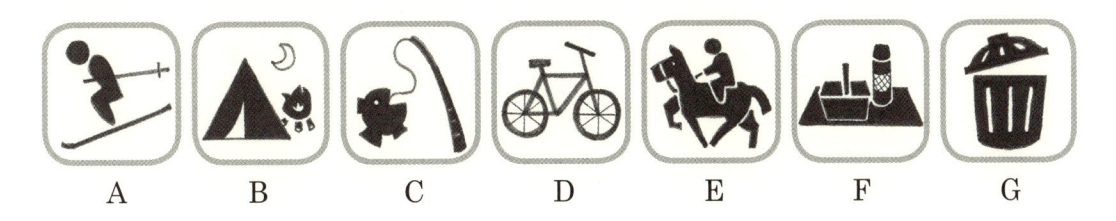

A   B   C   D   E   F   G

Students look at given symbols as shown above one by one, and guess what each of them corresponds to from the following list:
1. HORSEBACK RIDING;
2. GARBAGE CANS;
3. SKIING ;

4. CAMPING;
  5. PICNIC AREA;
  6. CYCLING;
  7. FISHING.

A time limit is needed for this game.

Materials for this activity come from authentic sources of information in media, so they are relevant to students' everyday lives. They can be found in legends in maps, guides, or pamphlets, such as those for sporting events, national parks, road maps, train lines and schedules, airport terminals, zoos, aquariums, and other public facilities.

Variation
- The teacher can have students find symbols of the same kind in the sources mentioned above and prepare those symbols for using in this game among students.

CHAPTER EIGHT

Classroom Dynamics

This chapter addresses classroom dynamics or classroom management with a view toward making English learning more successful through an effective classroom atmosphere. While recent years have ushered in many technological developments in education inconceivable 30 years ago, the only media of instruction readily accessible to teachers for centuries was "chalk and talk." Here, first, discussions will focus on the effectiveness of using the board and teacher talk. Next, pair and group work in language learning is taken into account, and finally, evaluation is discussed in detail.

§1 Optimal use of the board

The most versatile piece of classroom teaching equipment is the board, whether it is a conventional black or green chalk board, a whiteboard for use with markers, or an interactive whiteboard (IWB). Given that digital equipment is replacing conventional board use in some cases, teachers should still have the confidence that teaching can be done even with only a piece of chalk and the board.

For students, note-taking is the basis of learning and is greatly influenced by teachers' use of the board, to the extent that it is important for teachers to exploit basic techniques involved in its most effective use. The board provides a motivating central point for the whole class. What teachers do and do not write on the board can be a crucial factor for effective teaching.

In this section, the "whys" and "hows" of board-work are considered, based on the ideas disseminated and implemented by many teachers.

1 Purposes of board writing

The board can be used for various purposes. Some of these are as follows.

1) Aids for explanation
Teachers can use the board to explain target language items: vocabulary words, grammatical structures, and pronunciation. This helps students have a clear visual image of the main points.

2) Picture board

Teachers can draw simple sketches or diagrams to convey the messages more directly and explicitly. Pictures need not be elaborate. Stick figures, drawn carefully, convey the same amount of information as detailed pictures. The only limitation is artistic ability.

3) Student worksheet

Students can also use the board to write the answers to problems: a fill-in-the-blanks item, a sentence transformation, or a definition of a vocabulary word from the dictionary. This involves the entire class seeing what the correct version is.

4) Note board

Teachers can write words, phrases, grammatical items, and other items on the board that incidentally come up during classroom activities. Teachers may want students to remember or clearly understand those concepts over the course of the class.

5) Game square

Some word games involving vocabulary, for example, can be played on the board. Alternatively, when games are played competitively in teams, the board can be used as the score board. For this purpose, list the teams in a grid with their points beside them.

6) Notice board

Both teachers and students can write or affix to the board information and announcements for the entire class to see. The messages should be in English to encourage practical use of the language. The teacher can also display creative written works of students on the board for class sharing.

2 Effective use of the board

Above all, letters on the board should be neatly written in print rather than in script. Script is definitely for private correspondence and brief notes.

Here are some pointers on how to make the most efficient use of the board.

1) Before writing
- Start with a clean board. Each class should start with a clean slate. The board needs to be cleaned horizontally with an eraser, so that the faint lines marked on the board will help the teacher write letters beautifully along those lines.
- Split the board vertically (and horizontally when necessary) so that each area is dedicated to different entries: review of the week before,

class agenda, new words and/or phrases, or target grammar explanations.
- Plan to spend less time writing on the board, but make this time more effective. It is always worthwhile to pause to consider if given information can be provided in alternate ways. Cards and pictures can be useful alternatives and reused.
- Reserve enough space for teaching aids: flash cards, maps, pictures, and posters to lend authenticity and freshness to the class.
- Prepare board-work in advance and reflect on how best to use it to fulfill particular teaching goals.

2) While writing
- Write legibly in clear, large, and thick letters that are visible to everyone.
- Correct spelling and punctuation are obviously essential.
- Write capital letters clearly so that students see how they differ from small letters.
- Use colored chalk for emphasis, not for aesthetic effects.
- Refrain from using colors that do not stand out well on the board. Visibility decreases on the blackboard from yellow to red and to green, which is the least visible color.
- Do not talk to the board with your back turned to the class. This is demotivating and can make the class restless.
- Keep board-work properly organized. In other words, do not jot words, phrases, and sentences down in scrawls at random. This would bring nothing but confusion to your students.
- Clean the board when it becomes impossibly crowded, instead of squeezing in additional sentences wherever there is space.
- Involve learners with board-work as often as possible to keep them attentive to the classwork. This can be done with these techniques:
  - getting students to read a sentence as the teacher is writing it;
  - asking them how to spell difficult words or even what to write;
  - asking them to come to the board and write themselves.

3) After writing
- Go to the back row to check that the writing is easily legible to students seated farthest from it.
- Stand well away from the board so students can copy from the board or listen to explanations of what you have written.
- Face the class even while pointing to the board. Point backward, over your shoulder if necessary.
- Allow students sufficient time to copy from the board; do not erase the board too quickly.
- Wait patiently without speaking while students are busy copying; all the teacher's words become merely a jumble of sounds in their ears.

- To review the target items on the board, erase them gradually while confirming them as you proceed. For example, if the target is "She sells seashells by the seashore," first, erase the last three words and students repeat the entire original sentence after the model. Next, erase "seashells" (with only "She sells" remaining) and have them repeat the sentence again.

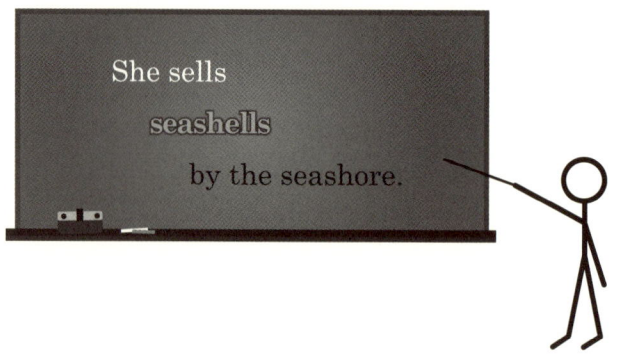

§2 Teacher talk

Teacher talk refers to the way teachers speak to the students in class. Here our discussion centers on teacher talk as skills to interact successfully with the class or individual students. Such classroom interaction enables teachers to do the following:

- make sure that students have correctly understood learning items before moving on to new topics;
- call attention to particular items under discussion;
- keep students actively participating in class.

From the perspectives above mentioned, we briefly discuss eliciting and questioning strategies.

1 Eliciting

What appears to be the problem with the following demonstration and how would you improve the scenario?

097: Teacher talk (1/8) Demonstration A

(*The teacher is reviewing the present continuous tense with a drawing on the board and a short mime.*)
T : (*pointing to the drawing where a boy is smiling*) Look, the boy is smiling. Yes, smiling. And it is spelled, (*spelling on the board*) "S-M-I-L-I-N-G." Next, watch me carefully.

(*miming picking up a phone and speaking into it*) I am calling. And it is spelled, "C-A-L-L-I-N-G."

This may be an extreme case, but it is obvious that the teacher speaks too much. He is rushing through the class. He may not have sufficient time to review the last class because of other things on the class agenda or on a shortened class schedule.

Regardless of the reasons, if the teacher monopolizes a large part of the class, students will become disengaged. Some may start to disrupt the class. This is an unproductive way to learn.

Wherein lies the difference between Demonstration A in the above and the following Demonstration B?

098: Teacher talk (2/8) Demonstration B

(*The scene is the same as Demonstration A.*)
T : (*pointing backward to the drawing where a boy is smiling*) Look, this boy is …Can you say it?
S$_1$: Smiling.
T : Yes, smiling. Good. How do you spell it? "S-"
S$_2$: "S-M-I-L-I-N-G."
T : (*spelling it on the board*) Yes, he is smiling. Good. Now, watch! (*miming picking up a phone and speaking into it*) I am…
S$_3$: Call.
T : Mmm… (*pointing to "ing" in the word "smiling" on the board*)
S$_3$: Calling.
T : Calling. Good. And it spells…
S$_4$: "C-A-L-L-I-N-G."

The difference is clear. Demonstration B is a perfect example of what is called eliciting or getting students to use knowledge at their command and inviting them to join in the learning process.

Eliciting is a series of actions: focusing students' attention, making them think, and encouraging them to draw on what they have experienced and what they know, or partly know. What is the use of eliciting in an English class?

Part of language learning is a process of working out new rules or remembering newly-learned rules. If the target word is "camel," the teacher can draw a picture on the board while saying, "It's a large desert animal with a long neck. You can ride on it." "Camel" may come from the class. That is how eliciting works.

Advantages of eliciting are as follows:

- better engaging students in learning;
- encouraging them to take more responsibility for their learning;
- making activities more relevant to their needs and interests;
- giving teachers opportunities to gauge how much they understand and adapt explanations to their level.

Without adequate elicitation, students may form the incorrect impression that everything they want to know will be spoon-fed to them, which is not the goal of education. The downside to elicitation, as the above examples clearly show, is that it is rather prone to take more time than direct presentation of a language item. Accordingly, most teachers, while admitting its merits, employ elicitation on a case-by-case basis.

2 Questioning strategies

Here two sets of questions are examined. They are based on opposing ideas: closed- or open-ended questions and display or referential questions. Other related issues are also dealt with.

1) Types of questions
<u>Closed- or open-ended questions</u>

Look at the first set of questions below, Types A and B. They are both about the content of a story entitled "Oh, my God, it's my son!" shown below. What distinguishes these question types?

099: Teacher talk (3/8) Question types (1/3)

Oh, my God, it's my son!
One day, a boy and his father went fishing on the river. They

> caught three big fish. The evening sky was darkening as they started to make their way home, and when they were almost halfway there, a bear came out of nowhere and attacked them. The father was killed on the spot, and the boy was injured. So he cried for help. Quickly, he was sent to the hospital. The doctor saw the boy and said, "Oh, my God, it's my son!"

Type A
Question 1:
    Where did they go fishing together?
Question 2:
    Where did the bear attack them?
Question 3:
    Why was the boy sent to the hospital?
Question 4:
    Was the doctor male or female?

Type B
Question 1:
    They didn't take back the fish. What do you think the reason was?
Question 2:
    Why do you think the father was killed and the boy was saved?
Question 3:
    How do you think the boy was sent to the hospital?
Question 4:
    How was the statement, "Oh, my God, it's my son!" possible in this context?

(Adapted from Davis and Rinvolucri, 1988:29-30)

For Type A questions, there is not much choice, either a single answer or just a limited variety of possible answers, which are usually short. Consequently, they are often referred to as **closed-ended**, or **convergent**, **questions**. In responding to students' answers to those questions, the teacher often follows up by stating whether the answer was correct. Such questions are good for listening practice and for a lead-in to learning how to answer questions in English, especially among beginning learners.

Additionally, closed-ended questions are mainly used to draw on students' previous knowledge about the materials and particular language items. Thus, the teacher may use the results to check the comprehension of the content or to test whether the target items have been understood. This information can be used for future course planning.

For Type B questions, what is required to answer, on the other hand, is rather different. There are no single right answers and may be no wrong ones, either. The questions are thought-provoking and various answers are possible. Therefore, they are called **open-ended**, or **divergent**, **questions**. Students are invited to freely express their ideas and opinions, which may sometimes defy the teacher's imagination.

Open-ended questions are intended to encourage learners to use any and all the language they know. Quite often, after students give answers, "follow-up" or "probe" questions may be asked. The only problem with this type of questions is that some students may become simply at a loss how to respond them owing to their complete unfamiliarity with this question type.

Open-ended questions are not only about the content of reading or listening comprehension materials as shown above. They are also about pictures or drawings in a course book as a mean of enhancing daily teacher student interaction.

Which type of questions is more beneficial? This may not be an either-or choice. However, the final goal of language teaching is for learners to develop better linguistic skills and abilities so they can maneuver successfully in real-life situations. Once we are clear about this, this consideration will help us make our decisions regarding this matter.

<u>Display or referential questions</u>
Look at the second set of questions below, Types C and D. How do the two types questions differ?

100: Teacher talk (4/8) Question types (2/3)

<u>Type C</u>
  T: Last week, we learned how to talk about the weather in English. <u>What is the weather like today?</u> Can anyone tell me? Haruka?
Haruka: Rainy and *heat*.
  T: It's rainy, Okay, and <u>*heat*, is it</u>? (*Someone says "Hot."*) Oh yes, hot.

<u>Type D</u>
  T: Good morning class. Let me take the roll. Oh, Shige isn't here. <u>Why is he absent today?</u>
Hiro: He's on his way.
  T: <u>How soon?</u>
Hiro: Five minutes *after*.
  T: Thank you, *in* five minutes.

The teacher often uses two types of questions demonstrated in the above.

The difference is obvious. Function of Type C questions such as "What is the weather like today?" and "…heat, is it?" is not to seek information. The answers to those questions are already known. The questions are not of practical importance and are posed merely to make students remember and review correct usage of the language describing weather conditions.

The function of Type D questions, "Why is he absent today?" and "How soon?" is to request information. The teacher wants to know why he is absent and how long it will be before he arrives. Those questions stem from practical necessity.

Type C and Type D questions are referred to as **display** and **referential questions**, respectively. It is true that each of them has its own functions and purposes, but it is quite clear which one communicates more authentic information than the other. Of the two types, referential questions are more often used in a communicative and real-life classroom setting.

Other related issues

Teachers should be careful not to direct questions repeatedly toward any particular student or group in class. It would be best to target questions all around the class, so that the entire class, strong or weak, feel involved. This is because in class, students primarily react to their teacher one-to-one in their minds. A teacher has a number of learners in one class, but each one has only one teacher to address.

Many teachers are unconsciously prone to address questions to one particular area in class. It may be the area where bright or active students are seated, or the front row or the right half in the classroom. Teachers with this tendency can overcome it with some practice. This is crucial for all students to feel actively engaged and motivated in the learning.

Here are two different ways of questioning. Which of the following two should be set as a model strategy, Type E or Type F?

101: Teacher talk (5/8) Question types (3/3)

Type E

    T: Hands up! What is the capital of France? (*Waits for a show of hands. Some hands shoot up.*) Okay, Nori.
Nori: Paris.

Type F

    T: Taka, what is the capital of the United States of America?
Taka: Washington, D.C.?

Type E is a better way to keep the whole class focused on the topic at hand, whereas in Type F the rest of the students will tune out as soon as they hear the teacher call on Taka. Moreover, in Type F, Taka may be startled to be abruptly called to answer the question. In addition, what would have happened if he did not know the right answer? He would have hated being asked like that, with the possibility of his losing confidence and self-esteem.

Therefore, generally, the teacher should first ask a question to the entire class and allow some time for students to think about it before choosing someone to answer.

Another question arises here. Suppose the teacher calls on Jane to reply to a question. At which position in the following diagrams should the teacher be located?

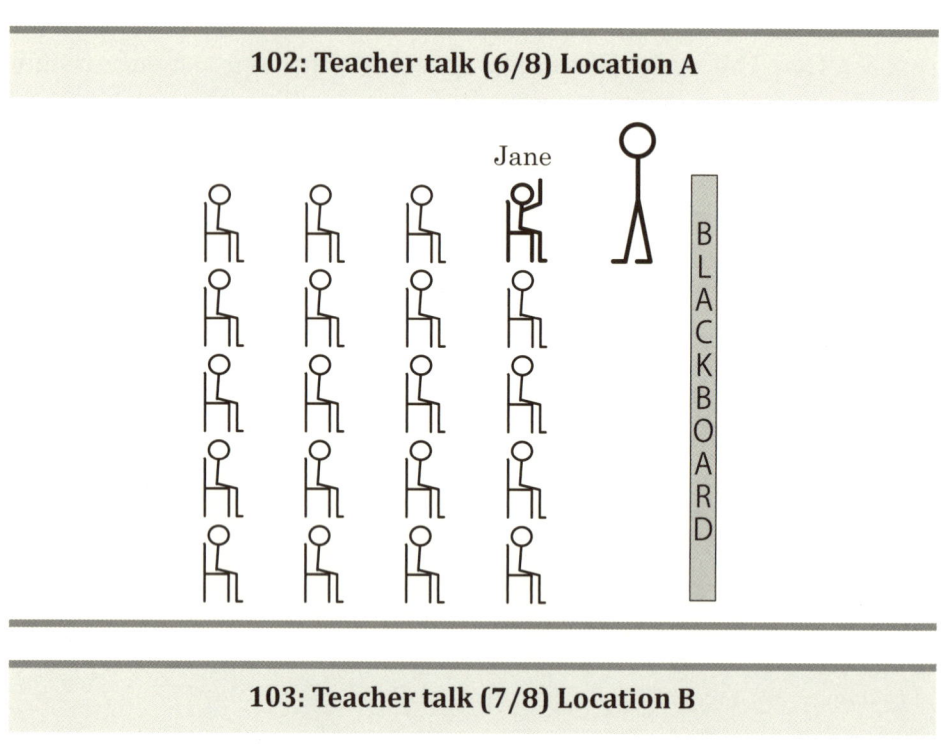

102: Teacher talk (6/8) Location A

103: Teacher talk (7/8) Location B

Location B shows a better position for the teacher. He should be ideally standing as far away as possible from Jane across the classroom. In this manner, the teacher's question to Jane and her answer can be heard more easily by the other students. Otherwise, some students will not be able to entirely participate in class. Thus, the teacher's place of standing in the classroom is significant for the effective use of questions and for better classroom management. This is particularly true when a class is rather large.

Consider the two responses from the teacher in the following scene. Which seems to be more effective to get the class involved in the lesson?

104: Teacher talk (8/8) Repeating right answers from students

Type G

(*The teacher gives a question to the class. Kay raises her hand and is called on.*)
Kay: (*giving her answer*) I think it is because of the weather.
T: Good. That's right. Now what would happen if…

Type H

(*the same situation*)
Yoshie: I think it is because of the weather.
T: (*looking over the class, in a loud voice*) Because of the weather. Good. That's right. Because of the weather. Now what would happen if…

In Type G, the teacher responds by saying, "Good. That's good," and proceeds with the lesson. However, the teacher in Type H responds, before anything else, by repeating the student's answer, which makes a big difference.

Particularly in a conventional classroom setting where the teacher responds to the class as a whole and its size is comparatively large, Type H should be taken as a model: It is unconceivable that all the other students are paying close attention to what the nominated student is supposed to say. The teacher should ensure that the whole class share the right answer and have the full understanding of the lesson content thus far, and then move on to the next lesson item.

As a rule, where the classroom situation is described as above, the teacher himself should repeat the student's right answer in a clear and loud voice, giving a nod of confirmation sign to the class. This action should be taken instantly before making any comments to the answer. Then the class would be more attentive and participate more with increased motivation.

However, we should expect or welcome cons of repeating answers from students. Some say that it will not facilitate learners' independence, which may be true of other different classroom settings.

§3 Pair work and group work

Many teachers now begin to recognize that learning between peers is just as important as the learning that occurs individually. Here we elaborate on pair work and group work in detail, along with some problems attendant on this issue.

1 Chief functions

A conventional picture of a classroom is the one where students sit neatly arranged in lines and a teacher stands in the front talking to them as a group. This is still the image of a typical classroom setting in many parts of the world. However, this teaching style has changed a great deal in the contemporary language-learning and -teaching environment.

A major reason is a shift in focus from grammar learning and memorization to a more communicative philosophy of language use. Students may learn, whether in isolation or in a whole class, both linguistic knowledge (structures, vocabulary) and skills with which to get information across. However, learning how to integrate these knowledge and skills for a real-life communicative purpose is quite another thing. It calls for quite a different approach, and pair or group work is the answer here.

Both pair and group work ensures that students in meaningful context use any and all the language they know. In doing this, students are relaxed taking language risks with their peers. Pair work lends itself well as a stepping stone to group work. Group work, in which the class get into groups of, for example, four or five, does not occur as frequently. However, it gives learners an extra edge over pair work in their opportunities to utilize linguistic knowledge in authentic application.

2 Side benefits

Some additional functions of pair or group work cannot be overlooked and are equally beneficial to learners. The first of these is the function of changing the classroom atmosphere. Teachers can choose from a variety of interaction patterns with the class. The most common is that in which the teacher simultaneously responds to them as a whole, or one where he controls and takes responsibility for all classroom activities. This is suitable for giving explanations and instructions. However, it gives students fresh impetus for the forthcoming classwork to switch to another mode of interaction (pair work or group work). This is particularly true for those who were not successful in the earlier sessions. In addition, listening to the teacher for a whole period places too much of a physical and mental burden on certain learners in some contexts, such as after a PE class or during the first class of the day.

Another advantage of pair or group work is that students will more actively join in and concentrate on the task. For example, if a certain topic is discussed in the whole-class format, only a few of the more outgoing students could dominate the discussion, while the others remain uninvolved.

An additional important advantage is that shy students feel more comfortable speaking their minds in small groups. They would thus be released from the pressure of the entire class listening to what they say. For those students, working in pairs and small groups is likely to serve as a springboard to their future speaking participation in front of the class.

Finally, the teacher has more chances to attend to the needs of special learners or groups, such as those who would not feel comfortable asking for help from the teacher engaging the whole class. They may feel more relaxed interacting with the teacher who is circulating during pair or group work.

3 Points to be observed

Pair work and group work sometimes create a problem unlikely to occur in a conventional class. Students may become noisy and some drift to completely irrelevant concerns. The risks of inviting unacceptable behaviors are greater than in a whole-class setting. Below are some tips to prevent the class from getting out of control.

1) Get into pairs with someone behind or in front

Pair work does not always have to involve two students sitting beside each other. Sometimes the partner could come from the row in front of or behind the student. That is, those who are sitting in the first and third rows turn around to work in pairs with those in the second and fourth rows. This arrangement is the perfect fit when the teacher does not want students to see each other's work.

2) How to organize a group

Students can split into different groups for different activities. They may get into groups with different skill levels (so that the more competent learners will help the others) or with others of the same skill level (so that they will meet suitable challenges). Alternatively, quiet and talkative persons can form groups (with a rule that each orally contributes to the task completion). The choice depends on the content and goal of the task.

Students can also be randomly organized into any number of groups the teacher wishes the class to split. If he has a class of 20 and needs five groups of four, he has the students count off in fives and groups all the "ones" into a group, all the "twos" in a group, and so forth.

3) Give directions step by step

It could be confusing and misleading for students to hear multiple sets of directions provided at the same time. Instructions should be broken down into simple steps that students can follow, that is, each step should be individually presented and at an appropriate moment. In case multiple directions need to be given simultaneously, they should be clearly written on the board.

4) What directions to give at what moment

Before an activity starts, a time limit has to be set to ensure that students concentrate on the task at hand. Some teachers may use music for this purpose and say, "Try to finish this before the music ends." The teacher should also announce what to do when the task is completed. He should say, for instance, "Return to your seat when finished" (if students are moving around in the classroom) or "Sit down when you are through" (if they are on their feet).

There are three advantages to telling what to do when a task is completed. First, some students may become restless and begin to interfere with the work of others, or start talking about irrelevant things if not told how to spend the extra time. Second, the teacher can tell who has finished or is still doing the task, though there is no need to wait for the whole class to complete it. Third, those who work more slowly will feel it necessary to complete the task faster when they see that other students have finished.

To start and end the activity, students need a clearly defined sign, for example, hand-clapping, ringing a call bell (the one seen on hotel desks), or blowing a whistle, so that the class will proceed at a brisk pace.

5) Circulate in the classroom

The teacher should go around the classroom, listening in on group discussions, clarifying directions, and providing guidance by asking questions. Walking around provides two other merits. First, the teacher can check the progress of students' performance, and second he observes the language use in the work, though the focal point is fluency rather than accurate language use.

If common or glaring errors are found, the teacher can remind the class afterward without mentioning names of the students who made them. This should not be done while the discussion is ongoing. It might well be to jeopardize the advantage of provoking fluent language use. He can also report and comment on model language usages overheard in class (here, students may be referred to by name).

When the teacher hears the students using their mother tongue, he should encourage, cajole, or help them use English. Learners that are more independent will contact him more willingly for his advice concerning language usages needed for the work.

6) Ask beforehand for students to present

The teacher should announce beforehand that some pairs or groups will be asked after the activity to come to the front and report to the class on what they discussed. First, this makes the class feel more responsible for their activities and helps them develop autonomy in their language learning. Second, presentations make it possible for the teacher to provide feedback. Finally, this provides another opportunity for authentic listening, since the remaining students will be anxious to hear what their peers have been doing.

7) Number each student in a group

In group work, particularly, there may be a student who depends on others to do the work and sits out during the assignment. If this is giving cause for concern, the teacher may have students number themselves off, say, from one to five (if they are in fives). He need not know who got which number. When the task is completed, the teacher chooses a number from one to five at random. Each student with that number will then report on the discussion from the group. Thus, everyone will be equally encouraged to participate actively in the work.

§4 Four types of test evaluations

Students in formal educational settings need to be tested on their English skills and abilities. Here we discuss four types of tests set at different stages of learning. Each of them has its own functions and features.

1 Placement tests

Placement tests are given when students enroll in a course. The tests are intended to group new students into teaching groups of appropriate levels, so that each learner receives teaching that is more adequate. These tests center on general ability rather than specific linguistic skills or items. Consequently, a single assessment cannot serve this purpose.

If a course aims to improve speaking skill, assessing the spoken language of applicants through an oral interview needs to be included in the test. In this manner, teachers know the following two aspects of a student's pronunciation skills. First, **accuracy** (how well English sounds are produced at segmental and suprasegmental levels) and second, **fluency** (how efficiently English sounds come out in a real communicative language use). The major concern must be how effectively students use language orally at the outset.

2 Diagnostic tests

Diagnostic tests, also referred to as progress tests, are set during the course of learning, at the end of each unit or lesson of the course book focused on certain language items. A function of these tests is to assess students' progress in learning particular items in the course. If the topic at hand is the present progressive tense, for instance, the test includes its meaning (in reference to present and past tenses), sentence structure and present participles of verbs.

When final results are available, the teacher should provide immediate feedback to the class. Positive outcomes give them fresh motivation for further learning. Not-so-positive outcomes provide useful information for the teacher and students as to what remedial work is required.

3 Achievement tests

Achievement tests, also called summative tests, are administered after a longer period of learning than diagnostic tests, for example, at the end of a term, a semester, or a school year. The purpose is to ensure that each student has met a certain criterion or to examine what level of performance s/he has reached in relation to their peers. Therefore, these tests cover a much wider range of topics than diagnostic tests. Indeed, they must reflect the entire contents of the course throughout. The results are a major factor in determining whether students receive the course certificate, take a make-up test, or repeat the course.

If such tests are carefully planned, their results may provide syllabus designers with valuable information for reorganizing and improving the course content.

4 Proficiency tests

Proficiency tests are used to check learners' ability at any time during the course of their learning. They serve to establish how much they have learned and what they can do with their knowledge. In other words, the main concern is the present command of the language in relation to their future needs. Thus, the test is required to include the type of language usage necessary in the situations that students will encounter. A career aptitude test is a case in point.

Suppose a student is planning to apply for a course in applied linguistics in an English-speaking country. The test this student takes should assess the mastery of basic vocabulary to discuss the discipline, ability to take notes, and organize the information for future research. All of these are needed for pursuing academic excellence.

REFERENCES

Applegate, R. (1975). The language teacher and the rules of speaking. *TESOL Quarterly 9*, 271-281.

Avery, P. & S. Ehrlich. (1995). *Teaching American English pronunciation*. Oxford: Oxford University Press.

Bartels, N. (2003). Written peer response in L2 writing. *English Teaching Forum 41* (1), 34-37.

Bourke, J. (2008). A rough guide to language awareness. *English Teaching Forum 46* (1), 12-21.

Brinton, D. (2001). The use of media in language teaching. In Celce-Murcia, M. (ed.) (2001). 459-476.

Canale, M. & M. Swain. (1980). Theoretical basis of communicative approaches to second language teaching and testing. *Applied Linguistics 1*, 1-47.

Celce-Murcia, M., D. Brinton & J. Goodwin. (2000). *Teaching pronunciation*. Cambridge: Cambridge University Press.

Celce-Murcia, M. (ed.) (2001). *Teaching English as a second or foreign language* 3rd. Boston, MA: Heinle & Heinle.

Cook, V. (1996). *Second language learning and language teaching* 2nd. London: Edward Arnold.

Crawford, M. (2005). Adding variety to word recognition exercises. *English Teaching Forum 43* (2), 36-41.

Cristal, D. (1997). *The Cambridge encyclopedia of the English language*. Cambridge: Cambridge University Press.

Csabay, N. (2006). Using comic strips in language classes. *English Teaching Forum 44* (1), 24-26.

Davis, P. & Rinvolucri, M. (1988). *Dictation: New methods, new possibilities*. Cambridge: Cambridge University Press.

DeFelice, W. (2012). Using story jokes for real communication. *English Teaching Forum 50* (3), 43-44.

Dobbs, J. (2001). *Using the board in the language classroom*. Cambridge: Cambridge University Press.

Doff, A. (1988). *Teach English: A training course for teachers*. Cambridge: Cambridge University Press.

Folse, K. (2008). Six vocabulary activities for the English language classroom. *English Teaching Forum 46* (3), 12-20.

Fry, E. (1989). *Skimming & scanning*. Blacklick, OH: Jamestown Publishers.

Grant, N. (1989). *Making the most of your textbook*. Essex: Longman.

Hadfirld, J. & C. Hadfirld. (2012). *Introduction to teaching English*. Oxford: Oxford University Press.

Harmer, J. (1998). *How to teach English: An introduction to the practice of English language teaching*. New York: Longman.

Harmer, J. (2007). *How to teach English*. Essex: Pearson/Longman.

Harmer, J. (2007). *The practice of English language teaching*. Essex: Pearson/

Longman.

Harrison, A. (1983). *A language testing handbook*. London: Macmillan.

Haycraft, J. (1999). *An introduction to English language teaching*. Essex: Longman.

Hill, L. (1980). *Introductory steps to understanding*. Oxford: Oxford University Press.

Iida, A. (2010). Developing voice by composing haiku: A social-expressivist approach for teaching haiku writing in EFL contexts. *English Teaching Forum 48* (1), 28-34.

Johnson, K. & H. Johnson. (ed.) (1999). *Encyclopedic dictionary of applied linguistics*. Oxford: Blackwell Publishers.

Jimbo, H. & R. Murto. (1990). *Paragraphs that communicate: Reading and writing paragraphs*. Tokyo: Linguaphone Japan.

Krashen, S. & T. Terrell. (1983). *The natural approach: Language acquisition in the classroom*. Oxford: Pergamon/Alemany.

Lindstromberg, S. (ed.) (2004). *Language activities for teenagers*. Cambridge: Cambridge University Press.

McCallum, G. (1980). *101 word games*. Oxford: Oxford University Press.

McCaughey, K. (2010). Ten great low-cost teaching tools. *English Teaching Forum 48* (4), 24-29.

McCaughey, K. (2013). Checklist talking. *English Teaching Forum 51* (2), 51-52.

Mahmoud, A. (2006). Translation and foreign language reading comprehension: A neglected didactic procedure. *English Teaching Forum 44* (4), 28-33.

Nation, P. (ed.) (1994). *New ways in teaching vocabulary*. Alexandria, VA: TESOL.

Okita, Y. (2004). *Eigokyoin no tame no jugyokatsudo to sono bunseki* [To analyze English classroom activities]. Kyoto: Showado.

Oshima, A. & A. Houge. (1988). *Introduction to academic writing*. Boston, MA: Addison-Wesley Publishing.

Pickett, J. et al. (2000). *The American heritage dictionary of the English language* 4th. Boston, MA: Houghton Mifflin Company.

Ramirez, M. (2012). The neglected tools can work for you. *English Teaching Forum 50* (4), 36-38, 45.

Richards, J., J. Platt & H. Platt. (1993). *Dictionary of language teaching & applied linguistics* 2nd. Essex: Longman.

Rinvolucri, M. (2005). Unleashing writing creativity in students. *English Teaching Forum 43* (4), 42-44.

Roell, C. (2010). Intercultural training with films. *English Teaching Forum 48* (2), 2-8.

Sakamoto, K. (1996). *Drop-formed island: A collection of haiku in English*. Kyoto: Eiden-sha.

Schindler, A. (2006). Channeling children's energy through vocabulary activities. *English Teaching Forum 44* (2), 8-12.

Shaptoshvili, S. (2002). Vocabulary practice games. *English Teaching Forum 40* (4), 34-37.

Shin, J. (2006). Ten helpful ideas for teaching English to young learners. *English Teaching Forum 44* (2), 2-7, 13.

Siegal, M. (2008). Sharing your vacation—send a postcard! *English Teaching Forum 46* (4), 51-56.

Soukhanov, A. et al. (1992). *The American heritage dictionary of the English language* 3rd. Boston, MA: Houghton Mifflin Company.

Tachibana, S. (2014). Creative writing—an approach to pronoun. *The English Teachers' Magazine 63* (7), 20-21.

Thornbury, S. (2005). *How to teach speaking.* Essex: Longman.

Wendy, A. & L. Ytreberg. (1990). *Teaching English to children.* Essex: Longman.

Wenxia, L. (2003). Teaching weak forms. *English Teaching Forum 41* (2), 32-35.

Widdowson, H. (1978). *Teaching language as communication.* London: Oxford University Press.

Williams, E. (1984). *Reading in the language classroom.* London: Macmillan.

Woods, C. (2005). *Teaching and assessing skills in foreign languages.* Cambridge: Cambridge University Press.

Yoshimura, I. & Abe, M. (2003). *Haiku no susume: Nihonjin no tame no eigohaiku nyuumon* [Introduction to haiku: A guide to English haiku for the Japanese]. Tokyo: Japan Times.

Zhang, Y. (2009). Reading to speak: Integrating oral communication skills. *English Teaching Forum 47* (1), 32-34.

Endangered species reading: Polar bear makes the list.(retrieved 2013/02/28) http://www.englishclub.com/reading/environment/endangered-species-reading.htm

How to use 4/3/2. (retrieved 2015/02/21) http://esolonline.tki.org.nz/ESOL-Online/Teacher-needs/Pedagogy/ESOL-teaching-strategies/Oral-language/4-3-2

INDEX

A

accuracy, 141
achievement tests, 142
acquisition-oriented listening, 9
active vocabulary, 68
assimilation, 98
audio-lingual method, 27, 28
authentic classwork, 75

B

back-chaining, 95
bottom-up listening, 13, 70
bottom-up reading, 48
brainstorming, 78

C

chants, 91
charades, 120
Classical Latin, 47
closed-ended (*or* convergent) questions, 133
coherence, 30
cohesion, 30
communicative activities, 31
communicative competence, 28
Communicative Language Teaching (CLT), 28
compound nouns, 90
content words, 91
conversational discourse, 30
couplets, 15

D

debate, 112
deductively (*or* deductive instruction), 10
diagnostic tests, 142
dictation, 18, 70
dicto-comp (*or* dicto-gloss), 69
discourse competence, 30
display questions, 135

E

EFL (English as a foreign language), 52
L1, 10
L2, 10
eliciting, 132

ESL (English as a second language), 52
extensive reading, 103

F

falling intonation, 94
flapped /t/, 96
fluency, 141
4/3/2 technique, 43
free writing, 79
function words, 91

G

General American English (GAE), 83
global errors, 84
gossip game, 89
Grammar Translation Method (GTM), 27, 47

H

haiku, 73

I

inauthentic classwork, 75
inductively (*or* inductive instruction), 10
information gap activities, 33
intensive reading, 103
inter-paragraph reading, 56
interview game, 34
intervocalic /t/, 96
intonation, 94
intra-paragraph reading, 56

J

jigsaw listening, 26
journal writing, 74

K

knock-knock joke, 99

L

learner autonomy, 77
learning-oriented listening, 12
lexical items, 13

lingua franca, 29, 74
linguistic competence, 29
linking, 97
listing, 78
local errors, 84

M

mapping, 80
metalanguage, 48
minimal pair, 86
minimal-pair practice, 27, 86

N

non-phonetic language, 18
nursery rhyme, 14

O

odd one out, 116
open-ended (*or* divergent) questions, 134

P

palatalization, 98
paragraph reading, 56
passive vocabulary, 68
past tense morphemes, 14
pattern practice, 27, 32
peer editing, 81
pictograph, 116
placement tests, 141
prepared speeches, 40
process approach, 77
product approach, 77
proficiency tests, 142
prominence, 92

Q

quick writing, 79

R

rapid reading, 56
read and look up, 102
realia, 10
Received Pronunciation (RP), 83

referential questions, 135
research project, 112
rhyming, 15
rhythm, 91
rising intonation, 94
role-play, 36

S

scanning, 60
schema, 20, 49
segmental features, 84
show and tell, 40
"Simon Says", 11
skimming, 56
sociolinguistic competence, 29
sound modifications, 96
speeches, 40
spelling bee, 120
spontaneous speeches, 41
strategic competence, 31
stress, 91
stress-timed language, 91
structure-based activities, 31
suprasegmental features, 84, 89
survey, 110
syllable-timed language, 91

T

tag questions, 94
task listening, 13, 24
teacher talk, 130
three-stage reading approach, 53
tongue twister, 87
top-down listening, 13, 18, 70
top-down reading, 48
Total Physical Response(TPR), 11

V

Vulgar Latin, 47

W

wet ink, 79

ACTIVITIES INDEX

Chapter One: On Listening
- 001: Total Physical Response 10
- 002: "Simon Says" 11
- 003: A conventional learning-oriented activity 12
- 004: Bottom-up listening (1/7) ("-ed" pronunciations) 13
- 005: Bottom-up listening (2/7) (stressed and unstressed words) 14
- 006: Bottom-up listening (3/7) (filling the blanks) 14
- 007: Bottom-up listening (4/7) (identifying words replaced with others or mispronounced) 15
- 008: Bottom-up listening (5/7) (finding discrepancies in a picture) 16
- 009: Bottom-up listening (6/7) (listening to the latest world weather in the news) 16
- 010: Bottom-up listening (7/7) (listening to plans for the summer) 17
- 011: Top-down listening (1/2) (rearranging pictures) 18
- 012: Top-down listening (2/2) (matching pictures) 20
- 013: Top-down and bottom-up listening combined (1/3) (using recorded materials) 21
- 014: Top-down and bottom-up listening combined (2/3) (using a real news broadcast) 22
- 015: Top-down and bottom-up listening combined (3/3) (using video clips) 23
- 016: Task listening (1/2) (picture dictation) 24
- 017: Task listening (2/2) (jigsaw listening) 25

Chapter Two: On Speaking
- 018: Pattern practice (1/2) (conventional type) 32
- 019: Pattern practice (2/2) (meaningful type) 32
- 020: Information gap activity (1/3) (collecting information from the peers) 34
- 021: Information gap activity (2/3) (collecting information about the teacher) 35
- 022: Information gap activity (3/3) (finding differences between the two) 36
- 023: Role-play (1/3) (continuing conversation) 37
- 024: Role-play (2/3) (holding imaginary conversations) 38
- 025: Role-play (3/3) (a husband and wife with different opinions) 39
- 026: Show and tell 40
- 027: Impromptu speech (1/3) (in pairs sitting behind or in front) 42
- 028: Impromptu speech (2/3) (4/3/2 technique) 43
- 029: Impromptu speech (3/3) (talking with a list) 44

Chapter Three: On Reading
- 030: Top-down reading and schema 50
- 031: Sample pre-reading activities 53
- 032: Sample during-reading activities 54
- 033: Sample post-reading activities 55
- 034: Logical development of one paragraph 57
- 035: Logical development of a short passage 58
- 036: Scanning 60

Chapter Four: On Writing
- 037: Copying sentences down from the board 65
- 038: Arranging and rewriting words 65
- 039: Changing words to match a picture 66
- 040: Imaginary writing 67
- 041: Constructing short sentences 68
- 042: Dicto-comp (1/2) (traditional type) 69
- 043: Dicto-comp (2/2) (interactive type) 70
- 044: Predicting the development of a passage 71
- 045: Filling in an empty cartoon "bubble" 72
- 046: Writing haikus 73
- 047: Journal writing 73
- 048: Writing to a host family 74
- 049: Completing an application form 75
- 050: Process approach>getting started>listing 78
- 051: Process approach>getting started>brainstorming 78

Activities index

    052: Process approach>getting started>quick writing 79
    053: Process approach>getting started>mapping 79
    054: Process approach>proofreading 80

Chapter Five: On Pronunciation
    055: Snow White Joke 84
    056: Segmental (1/7) (aspiration of stop voiceless sounds) 85
    057: Segmental (2/7) (minimal-pair practice: voiced or voiceless consonants) 85
    058: Segmental (3/7) (minimal-pair practice: difficult sounds) 86
    059: Segmental (4/7) (minimal-pair practice: "a cap" or "a cup") 87
    060: Segmental (5/7) (with the help of realia in a meaningful context) 88
    061: Segmental (6/7) (in the context) 88
    062: Segmental (7/7) (in a gossip game) 89
    063: Suprasegmental (1/7) (stressed words: GREEN house or green HOUSE) 90
    064: Suprasegmental (2/7) (stress and rhythm: with the help of "chants") 91
    065: Suprasegmental (3/7) (prominence: stress on emphasized words) 92
    066: Suprasegmental (4/7) (prominence: stress on new information) 92
    067: Suprasegmental (5/7) (intonation patterns in tag questions) 93
    068: Suprasegmental (6/7) (intonation patterns: three types) 94
    069: Suprasegmental (7/7) (back-chaining) 95
    070: Flapping of the intervocalic /t/ 96
    071: Linking 97
    072: Assimilation 98
    073: Knock-knock jokes 99

Chapter Six: On Integration
    074: Repeating a group of sentences in different words 102
    075: Asking questions in pairs 102
    076: As a post-reading activity 103
    077: Impersonation of a main character 104
    078: Using a comic strip 106
    079: Applying for an EFL program 107
    080: Newspaper reporting 107
    081: Postcard writing 108
    082: Conducting a survey 110
    083: Group research project 111
    084: Debate 112

Chapter Seven: Vocabulary Games
    085: Pictograph 116
    086: Odd one out 116
    087: Hidden commonalities 117
    088: Animal grid 118
    089: Spelling bee 120
    090: Charades 120
    091: Scrambled words 121
    092: Missing vowels 122
    093: Secret code 123
    094: Key words 123
    095: Words within a word 124
    096: Matching symbols with meanings 125

Chapter Eight: Classroom Dynamics
    097: Teacher talk (1/8) Demonstration A 130
    098: Teacher talk (2/8) Demonstration B 131
    099: Teacher talk (3/8) Question types (1/3) 132
    100: Teacher talk (4/8) Question types (2/3) 134
    101: Teacher talk (5/8) Question types (3/3) 135
    102: Teacher talk (6/8) Location A 136
    103: Teacher talk (7/8) Location B 136
    104: Teacher talk (8/8) Repeating right answers from students 137

To Learn How to Teach English
With Practical Classroom Activities

Copyright © 2015 by OKITA, Yoshio

All rights reserved.

No part of this book may be reproduced in any form or by any means without permission in writing from the author.

Kwansei Gakuin University Press
1-1-155 Uegahara, Nishinomiya, Hyogo, 662-0891, Japan
ISBN: 978-4-86283-207-8

著者紹介

大喜多 喜夫（おおきた・よしお）

高等学校英語科教諭、大阪府科学教育センター（現大阪府教育センター）指導主事研兼究員を経て、関西学院大学教授。テンプル大学大学院修士課程修了。著書として『英語教員のための応用言語学』（昭和堂 2000）、『英語教員のための授業活動とその分析』（昭和堂 2004）などがある。

To Learn How to Teach English
With Practical Classroom Activities

2015 年 9 月 30 日初版第一刷発行

著　者　大喜多喜夫

発行者　田中きく代
発行所　関西学院大学出版会
所在地　〒 662-0891
　　　　兵庫県西宮市上ケ原一番町 1-155
電　話　0798-53-7002

イラスト　オオヒラ航多
印　刷　株式会社遊文舎

©2015 OKITA, Yoshio
Printed in Japan by Kwansei Gakuin University Press
ISBN 978-4-86283-207-8
乱丁・落丁本はお取り替えいたします。
本書の全部または一部を無断で複写・複製することを禁じます。